Spiritual Exhaustion
By Julie Anshasi

Giant Publishing Company
Lincoln, Nebraska, USA

2021 by Julie Anshasi

Published by Giant Publishing Company
Post Office Box 6455
Lincoln, NE 68506
www.giantpublishingcompany.com

Printed in the United States of America

Cover photo courtesy of Microsoft Office Clip Art

All scripture quotations are from the King James Version of the Bible, unless otherwise noted.

Library of Congress Cataloging-in-Publication Data
Anshasi, Julie, 1963 -
Spiritual Exhaustion   self-help/Julie Anshasi
    1. Christianity
    2. Self-help
TX0008966387

ISBN 978-1-7352827-1-8

For the Odoys

Therefore, my beloved brethren, be ye stedfast, unmoveable, always abounding in the work of the Lord, forasmuch as ye know that your labour is not in vain in the Lord. 1 Corinthians 15:58

Books by Julie Anshasi

Broken ~ Poems from the Holy Spirit
Copyright 2017 – Winner of the 2021 Illumination
Book Awards Silver Medal

Some Things are HOT! Some Things are NOT!
Copyright 2018

Behind the Word: Bible Stories to Ignite Your Imagination
Copyright 2018

Why Did the Dinosaurs Die?
Copyright 2019

Winter in Eden
Copyright 2020 – Winner of the 2022 Illumination
Book Awards Bronze Medal

The Revelation of Jesus Christ
Copyright 2020

One Part Nonsense
Copyright 2020

Forgiving Yourself
Copyright 2021

Table of Contents

Chapter 1: How much longer, Lord?..................……Page 1

Chapter 2: Broken…………………………………….…Page 3

Chapter 3: Church……………………………..……...Page 7

Chapter 4: Praying…………..................……..……Page 13

Chapter 5: Reading the Bible……………….........…Page 22

Chapter 6: Doing good works………………...…..Page 26

Chapter 7: The wrong place at the wrong time……..Page 32

Chapter 8: Sin…………………………………….....Page 40

Chapter 9: Rebellion………………………...........Page 50

Chapter 10: Guilty conscience………………………Page 59

Chapter 11: False guilt …………………………....Page 63

Chapter 12: If only…………………………………...Page 68

Chapter 13: Rebuking the devourer……………….Page 71

Chapter 14: Psychology..……………………………Page 75

Chapter 15: The latest thing……………………......Page 83

Chapter 16: Speaking the word of God……………..Page 89

Chapter 1: How much longer, Lord?

I lie in bed, staring at the ceiling. I am very tired, but can't sleep. This is, unfortunately, a common occurrence.

My mind wanders back over the events of the past few years. I remind God of a few things that I think, perhaps, He has forgotten.

It's coming up on ten years, God. Ten years. You promised me. You told me what was going to happen. I have done what You asked me to do, to the best of my ability. Have I failed You in some way? Is there something I forgot to do? Please don't forget about me, God. I need the fulfilment of Your word in my life.

The daylight hours are usually not a problem for me. I keep very busy with my day job, and evenings are either spent in church, or writing. I remember what He had told me a few years earlier, regarding my writing. I had cried out to Him in desperation.

Please, God. Please give me something to do while I'm waiting.

He had gently reminded me of the talent I had buried in the earth (Matthew 25:14-30) for so many years. I had been writing since I was a young child, but never did anything other than shove one filled notebook after another under my bed, or worse, toss them into the trash.

After His gentle reminder, I had begun writing in earnest, and published several books, and even won a national writing award. I knew the ability to write came from Him, not me, because when I read back over things that I have written, I am astonished at the insights recorded on the pages. I thank God for the gift He's given me.

Yes, the daylight hours are usually okay. But every night, when I climb into my bed, alone, with the natural darkness surrounding my house, and the spiritual darkness oppressing my soul, inevitably the tears and the questions come.

I've tried, Lord. You know I've tried. Have I missed something? Have You changed Your mind?

As a Christian, my mind knows that I am not in spiritual darkness.

The people that walked in darkness have seen a great light: they that dwell in the land of the shadow of death, upon them hath the light shined. Isaiah 9:2

But, my heart sometimes tells me that I am.

I think about Abraham. God told him he would have a son. Twenty-five years later, he did. My flesh recoils at the thought of this.

Is it going to take twenty-five years? I don't think I can wait that long, God. It seems to me that I am dying already. Twenty-five years? I'll never make it.

The tears slide down the sides of my face, and my pillowcase is wet, again. But eventually, sleep always takes over. Tomorrow is a new day, right? Things will be better tomorrow….

They have to be.

Chapter 2: Broken

"The night I sailed for China, March 3, 1893, my life, on the human side, was broken, and it never was mended again." Amy Carmichael

"We are not necessarily doubting that God will do the best for us; we are wondering how painful the best will turn out to be." C.S. Lewis

"The most terrible poverty is loneliness, and the feeling of being unloved." Mother Teresa

I knew intellectually, of course, that my life was no different from thousands of other lives. Everyone has a cross to bear, even the non-Christian, although he doesn't recognize it as a cross. But that intellectual knowledge didn't make things any easier. Like the saints quoted above, I felt that my life was broken and unmended. I was wondering how much more pain God would put on me in order to achieve His best. And, always, I suffered from unbearable loneliness.

As Christians, we know that God must break us, melt us, and re-shape us, in order to use us. There's even a song about that. So, we do our best to submit to His pounding of ourselves, the clay that He has created for His purposes.

The word which came to Jeremiah from the LORD, saying, Arise, and go down to the potter's house, and there I will cause thee to hear my words. Then I went down to the potter's house, and, behold, he wrought a work on the wheels. And the vessel that he made of clay was marred in the hand of the potter: so he made it again another vessel, as seemed good to the potter to make it. Then the word of the LORD came to me, saying, O house of Israel, cannot I do with you as this potter? saith the LORD. Behold, as the clay is in the potter's hand, so are ye in mine hand, O house of Israel. Jeremiah 18:1 - 6

You and I will never be what God wants us to be, unless we submit to His pounding. I am using the word "pounding" deliberately. If you have ever made anything out of clay, you know that you start with a formless lump that looks like nothing, and you begin forming it into what you want it to be. You press it, you pound it flat on the table, you pick it up and start pinching it. Sometimes, somewhere along the process, you realize that it doesn't look at all as you had originally planned for it to look, so you crush it back into a formless lump once more, and begin again.

The clay has no feelings. It doesn't care one way or another how many times you crush it and start pinching it again. But you and I have feelings. Even though we are made of dirt (clay), we have feelings!

And the LORD God formed man of the dust of the ground, and breathed into his nostrils the breath of life; and man became a living soul. Genesis 2:7

It hurts so much to be continually crushed. We may look in our (spiritual) mirror and see a pretty nice-looking guy or gal, and wonder why God has to keep crushing and re-forming us.

For whom he did foreknow, he also did predestinate to be conformed to the image of his Son, that he might be the firstborn among many brethren. Romans 8:29

God could have simply created us from our conception in the image of Jesus Christ, thereby skipping the crushing process. But in order for us to be conformed to the image of His son, we have to be molded into that image. This dirty clay, which

4

has the form of sin, has to be molded, transformed, and conformed to become something else.

Behold, I was shapen in iniquity; and in sin did my mother conceive me. Psalm 51:5

Injustice

When we see something that is wrong, we want God to make it right. That is the universal human condition.

How long wilt thou forget me, O LORD? forever? how long wilt thou hide thy face from me? Psalm 13:1

O LORD, how long shall I cry, and thou wilt not hear! even cry out unto thee of violence, and thou wilt not save! Habakkuk 1:2

And they cried with a loud voice, saying, How long, O Lord, holy and true, dost thou not judge and avenge our blood on them that dwell on the earth? Revelation 6:10

Waiting for justice can break you down. My pastor once said that while waiting for a breakthrough, you can have a breakdown.

But (Elijah) himself went a day's journey into the wilderness, and came and sat down under a juniper tree: and he requested for himself that he might die; and said, It is enough; now, O LORD, take away my life; for I am not better than my fathers. And as he lay and slept under a juniper tree, behold, then an angel touched him, and said unto him, Arise and eat. 1 Kings 19:4-5

Elijah was a broken man. He was crushed in spirit. All he wanted to do was to die. That's when God ministered to him.

God breaks us in ways that we can't imagine, using methods that make no sense, from the human perspective. C.S. Lewis put it this way:

"Imagine yourself as a living house. God comes in to rebuild that house. At first, perhaps, you can understand what He is doing. He is getting the drains right and stopping the leaks in the roof and so on; you knew that those jobs needed doing and so you are not surprised. But presently He starts knocking the house about in a way that hurts abominably and does not seem to make any sense. What on earth is He up to? The explanation is that He is building quite a different house from the one you thought of - throwing out a new wing here, putting on an extra floor there, running up towers, making courtyards. You thought you were being made into a decent little cottage: but He is building a palace. He intends to come and live in it Himself."
C.S. Lewis, Mere Christianity

I have seen that Jesus Christ is beautiful. He is the most beautiful thing that any human being could ever desire. He, being sinless, still had to be crushed by the Father!

But he was wounded for our transgressions, he was bruised for our iniquities: the chastisement of our peace was upon him; and with his stripes we are healed. Isaiah 53:5

If He had to be, why should I think I don't have to be? The reality is, if I want Him, I do have to be.

"The Lord annihilates the Christian, only to transform him into Himself." Jeanne Guyon

Chapter 3: Church

I am standing up front, clutching the microphone, singing my heart out. I don't know how I ended up singing with the worship leaders, other than by default. I'd describe my singing voice as average, at best. But one by one the beautifully talented singers drifted away, either from the church or into other ministry areas, and a spot had to be filled, so I filled it.

A lot of times I really don't feel like singing. But I am learning that the Christian life doesn't have much to do with how I feel. It's all about Him.

Sometimes I pray as I am on my way to fellowship with the other believers. *Lord, please let my singing glorify You today. Please let it be a sweet-smelling savor to You. I want to please You, Lord. I don't care what anyone else thinks about my singing; I want You to be happy with it! Thank You, Jesus.*

So, I sing, and dance, and lift my hands to Him. He is worthy of all my praise and my very best efforts, no matter how pitiful they seem to me.

I thank God for my church. I thank God for the pastors, a husband-and-wife team, who have poured themselves body and soul into this little band of believers. So many times, I have seen them arrive with exhaustion all over their faces, and I know that once again they have been up all night, praying about some situation, or for someone in the church. Sometimes that someone is me! I am continually humbled at their love for me, and for all of us. I cannot imagine my life without these people that I love so much.

Whenever the church doors are open, I am there. Satan does his very best to try to prevent me from being there, which is simply confirmation to me that it is the place I need to be. For example:

One Sunday I was getting ready for church, and rushing around, as usual. I looked down at the floor and realized that my cat had apparently had some sort of digestive issue during the night. The smell was overpowering and repulsive. I quickly cleaned up the mess, only to discover another mess. And another, and another, and another. My bed was contaminated, as was the guest room bed, the downstairs couch, some pillows, rugs, and pretty much every floor in every room. I stood, staring in disbelief at the shape my house was in. I had two thoughts, in rapid succession. Number one: *There is no way I will be able to go to church today. This will take hours to clean up.* Number two: *I'll just leave, and clean it all up when I get back.*

I quickly rejected both thoughts. Instead, I prayed.

Lord, You know how much I want to go to church today. Please, somehow, let me get this cleaned up and get to church on time.

I got to work with my rag and bucket. The washing machine hummed. I tried not to look at the clock. *If I walk in late, at least that's better than not going at all,* I thought.

But I didn't walk in late. God supernaturally stretched time and allowed me to get everything cleaned up, thoroughly, and I walked in the door exactly on time. I know, in the natural realm, this was completely impossible. But what is impossible with man, is possible with God (Luke 18:27).

I really pulled the rug out from under Satan that day. He had laid a trap for me, intending to divert me from church, but he failed miserably, because he is a liar and a loser.

Satan will use anything to keep you from being in church. I have heard many couples testify that right before they are heading out the door on Sunday morning, they get into an argument, or one of their children misbehaves, or the dog runs away. Satan wants us to throw up our hands and say, "I can't go to church today!" And that is what I almost said, the morning of the "cat-astrophe." (Sorry, I couldn't resist that pun.) Thankfully the Lord intervened and I was able to see what was really happening, and made up my mind that I was going to church, no matter what.

When you are at the end of your spiritual rope, you need the body of Christ.

For the body is not one member, but many. If the foot shall say, Because I am not the hand, I am not of the body; is it therefore not of the body? And if the ear shall say, Because I am not the eye, I am not of the body; is it therefore not of the body? If the whole body were an eye, where were the hearing? If the whole were hearing, where were the smelling? But now hath God set the members every one of them in the body, as it hath pleased him. And if they were all one member, where were the body? But now are they many members, yet but one body. And the eye cannot say unto the hand, I have no need of thee: nor again the head to the feet, I have no need of you. Nay, much more those members of the body, which seem to be more feeble, are necessary: And those members of the body, which we think to be less honourable, upon these we bestow more abundant honour; and our uncomely parts have more abundant comeliness. For our comely parts have no need: but God hath tempered the body together, having given more abundant honour to that part which lacked. That there should be no schism in the body; but that the members should have the same care one for another. And whether one member suffer, all the members suffer with it; or one member be honoured, all the members rejoice with it. Now ye are the body of Christ, and members in particular. 1 Corinthians 12:14-27

I love these verses that explain what the church should be. He is the head, and we are the body. God made our human bodies to work in such a marvelous and miraculous way! I never have to wonder what my liver is doing, or if my blood is circulating at the proper speed. Each part of my body performs its own function flawlessly, and no part is in competition with any other part. The very thought of that is ridiculous.

The members of the body of Christ need one another! Satan always tries to isolate and separate us from each other, telling us that we don't need one another, don't need to go to fellowship gatherings, etc. He uses petty little differences, and they are almost always petty, to separate us from one another and to put up emotional walls between members.

That there should be no schism in the body; but that the members should have the same care one for another. And whether one member suffer, all the members suffer with it; or one member be honoured, all the members rejoice with it. 1 Corinthians 12:25-26

The Lord does not want a schism in His body. A schism is a crack, or a division. He wants us to remain united, whole, and complete.

So many things in the Christian life are counter-intuitive. When you are physically exhausted, you naturally want to rest. When you are spiritually exhausted, you often feel that you need to take a break from church, from spiritual activities, and from other people. But that is the worst thing you can do!

Not forsaking the assembling of ourselves together, as the manner of some is; but exhorting one another: and so much the more, as ye see the day approaching. Hebrews 10:25

One of the purposes of meeting together is to exhort one another. When I am down, a brother or sister has the right word to give me, and vice versa.

It is a very short journey from spiritual exhaustion to spiritual isolation, to spiritual deadness.

I see my pastors, day after day, and year after year, forgoing sleep for prayer, forgoing food for fasting, and forgoing their own hopes and dreams for His kingdom. When I am feeling especially down, I remind myself that if they can do it, I can do it too, by the grace of God.

Some people are spiritually exhausted because they try to do everything in the church. Don't try to be the gardener, security officer, hospitality chairperson, Sunday school teacher, custodian, usher, worship leader, childcare worker, and sound technician all at the same time. Trust me, that will guarantee exhaustion. But find one or two things that need to be done for the church, and do them very well. Many times, when I don't feel like going to church, I remember that there are certain tasks that I have agreed to do, and I realize that I am needed, so I go. I am always blessed by going.

Stay in the body of Christ, no matter how difficult it may become to stay there! Yes, it's true, sometimes the Lord does tell us to leave a particular fellowship and become a part of another one, but too many times, when the going gets tough, the believer drops out. God never intended that for His people.

Chapter 4: Praying

And I say unto you, Ask, and it shall be given you; seek, and ye shall find; knock, and it shall be opened unto you. For every one that asketh receiveth; and he that seeketh findeth; and to him that knocketh it shall be opened. Luke 11:9-10

If a son shall ask bread of any of you that is a father, will he give him a stone? or if he ask a fish, will he for a fish give him a serpent? Luke 11:11

Pray without ceasing. 1 Thessalonians 5:17

After following the Lord for many years, you would think I would thoroughly understand prayer. But, I don't.

Lord, would You please just answer my prayer? Even "no" would be an answer. That's not what I want to hear, but at least if You said no, I could close the door on this and move on to something else.

I remember my childhood. I was a naughty child. In the grocery store with my mother, I would pester that poor woman to no end. I wanted her to buy the latest sugary cereal, salty junk food, many various flavors of gourmet ice cream, and on and on. I wonder why she continued to take me with her.

My own son, in contrast, never asked for anything in the grocery store. In this and many other ways, he was an unusual child.

One day in church, I sat across from the pastor. "Pastor Racheal," I asked, my eyes cast down and brimming with tears. "Is God tired of my constant asking for the same thing?

My mom always used to say, 'If you ask me one more time, you'll get a spanking.' Is God losing His patience with me?"

She smiled her usual gentle smile. "Don't stop asking Him," she said simply. "He never gets tired of us asking Him."

He doesn't get tired, but we get tired.

Prayer is hard work. It seems like it should be easy, but it's not. I've heard it said that prayer does not convince God to give us anything; rather, it aligns our wishes with His. As we pray, His will for our lives is revealed, and our prayers come around to His side, so to speak. Maybe that's why, after almost ten years of praying for the same thing, I have never been able to stop.

Oh, I have wanted to stop. I have tried to stop. On particularly low days, I have been unable to pray at all. My prayers simply dissolve into tears.

I am weary with my groaning; all the night make I my bed to swim; I water my couch with my tears. Psalm 6:6

But through His supernatural power, when morning comes, He strengthens me to pray again.

I remember Job.

And the LORD turned the captivity of Job, when he prayed for his friends: also the LORD gave Job twice as much as he had before. Job 42:10

Job was in captivity – prison – because of his situation. He was not in an actual prison, but he had no freedom. His health was gone, along with every material possession. I believe he owned the clothes on his back, and that was it.

Job exhausted every possible reason in his mind as to why he was in the condition he was in. Was it because of sin? Was there hidden pride in his life? Did God just stop liking him?

The Bible tells us that Job came out of his mental prison when he prayed for his friends. He reminds me of this, often, and reminds me of the people who need prayer. So, I pray for them.

In every fellowship group, there are hurting people. You really don't have to look very far! I am astonished when I hear the stories in my own church about accidents, disease, sickness, job loss, infidelity, abandonment, domestic violence, imprisonment (this time in an actual prison), homelessness, addiction – you name it. Not to mention witchcraft, voodoo, and demonic possession.

Satan hasn't somehow become a nicer guy over the centuries. If anything, he is more wicked now than when he was first cast out of heaven.

Lest Satan should get an advantage of us: for we are not ignorant of his devices. 2 Corinthians 2:11

It simply doesn't do you or me any good to close our eyes and pretend Satan isn't there. I can assure you, he is there, and he hates us with vitriolic hatred.

For we wrestle not against flesh and blood, but against principalities, against powers, against the rulers of the darkness of this world, against spiritual wickedness in high places. Ephesians 6:12

But what about unanswered prayer?

And this is the confidence that we have in him, that, if we ask any thing according to his will, he heareth us... 1 John 5:14

After many, many years of praying for a child, Abraham decided to take matters into his own hands. He fathered a child, Ishmael, through an ungodly relationship with a woman who was not his wife, and his wife actually encouraged him to do this (Genesis 16). The entire world has been in turmoil ever since, because two people got tired of waiting for the fulfillment of God's promise.

I don't know about you, but this gives me pause. Ishmael, to us, represents missing the mark. He represents discarding God's will and plan in favor of our own.

Yes, I want God to answer my prayer, and yes, I want Him to answer it today. Having waited ten years already, I don't want to wait another fifteen.

But I don't want Ishmael! A well-meaning person, who I respect and love, actually told me that I should go ahead and get Ishmael (figuratively speaking), because God is merciful, and He would bless my life in spite of my wrong decision, just as He blessed Abraham and Ishmael. I had to bite my tongue, because "Get behind me, Satan" was about to come out of my mouth, and that would not have helped my future relationship with this person. This person told me that if I was truly doing God's will, I would not be shedding tears over it; instead, I would be happy and joyful.

But the Bible tells a different story. Jesus Himself had an opportunity to settle for Ishmael instead of God's plan for His life. He chose God's plan, and He shed a lot of tears.

We read these accounts in Luke and Matthew, recording what Jesus went through right before His crucifixion.

16

And being in an agony he prayed more earnestly: and his sweat was as it were great drops of blood falling down to the ground. Luke 22:44

Then cometh Jesus with them unto a place called Gethsemane, and saith unto the disciples, Sit ye here, while I go and pray yonder. And he took with him Peter and the two sons of Zebedee, and began to be sorrowful and very heavy. Then saith he unto them, My soul is exceeding sorrowful, even unto death: tarry ye here, and watch with me. And he went a little farther, and fell on his face, and prayed, saying, O my Father, if it be possible, let this cup pass from me: nevertheless not as I will, but as thou wilt. And he cometh unto the disciples, and findeth them asleep, and saith unto Peter, What, could ye not watch with me one hour? Watch and pray, that ye enter not into temptation: the spirit indeed is willing, but the flesh is weak. He went away again the second time, and prayed, saying, O my Father, if this cup may not pass away from me, except I drink it, thy will be done. And he came and found them asleep again: for their eyes were heavy. And he left them, and went away again, and prayed the third time, saying the same words. Then cometh he to his disciples, and saith unto them, Sleep on now, and take your rest: behold, the hour is at hand, and the Son of man is betrayed into the hands of sinners. Rise, let us be going: behold, he is at hand that doth betray me. And while he yet spake, lo, Judas, one of the twelve, came, and with him a great multitude with swords and staves, from the chief priests and elders of the people. Matthew 26:36-47

These accounts of Jesus spiritually wrestling with God are fascinating, sobering, and thought-provoking. Jesus knew God's will for His life. He knew that God wanted Him to be executed for a crime He didn't commit. Shortly before He prayed in the garden of Gethsemane, He had explained to his disciples what God's plan for Him was.

From that time forth began Jesus to shew unto his disciples, how that he must go unto Jerusalem, and suffer many things of the elders and chief priests and scribes, and be killed, and be raised again the third day. Matthew 16:21

Yet it pleased the LORD to bruise him; he hath put him to grief: when thou shalt make his soul an offering for sin, he shall see his seed, he shall prolong his days, and the pleasure of the LORD shall prosper in his hand. Isaiah 53:10

Yes, Jesus knew God's will for His life, and He was willing to choose God's very best for Him, even though He didn't want to!

Father, if this cup may not pass away from me, except I drink it, thy will be done. Matthew 26:42b

The Bible doesn't tell us what Jesus wanted instead of the cross. I heard a wise man of God say once that Jesus wanted to defeat the devil, there and then, instead of leaving His followers to fight the battle with Satan.

I have learned that God always answers our prayers. I have also learned that He rarely answers them in the timeframe we would like Him to.

My church recently went through a time of intense prayer and fasting, for a specific purpose. We felt the urgency of the situation and knew that the church had to rise up to combat the supernatural forces of evil that were trying to take over. We prayed and fasted, and prayed and fasted some more. We knew we were joining many other churches across the country who were doing the same thing.

The situation didn't turn out in our favor, to put it mildly.

After this incident, I stood in church one Thursday evening before Bible study was about to start. Tears streamed down my face as my pastor spoke gently to me. I kept interrupting him. I finally told him that I didn't want to hear any more. We had all prayed and fasted, and what good had it done? It seemed obvious to me that God had washed His hands of the situation.

That evening, God spoke in His still, small voice. He reminded us that even though things looked absolutely hopeless, He still had a plan, and His plan would amaze and confound everyone. He had heard our prayers, and was answering them, and in His way that only He understands, He was answering them at a time when all hope had been lost.

Even though I absolutely could not understand what had happened, I knew that I had to cling to God and His promises to His people. What other choice did I have?

I have seen too many people walk away from the Lord because things didn't go their way. And the scripture is never wrong. When you walk away, your life becomes much more hopeless than you felt it was when you didn't see your prayer answered.

Holding faith, and a good conscience; which some having put away concerning faith have made shipwreck… 1 Timothy 1:19

This is a vivid word picture. When a ship has wrecked, it is lying in pieces on the water. The people who were in it have either drowned, or are clinging desperately to bits of wreckage. This is what happens to your life and mine when we "put away" our faith. You do not know, dear saint, how many people you are carrying. If your faith becomes shipwrecked, they could drown along with you.

But whoso shall offend one of these little ones which believe in me, it were better for him that a millstone were hanged about his neck, and that he were drowned in the depth of the sea. Matthew 18:6

G.K. Chesterton said that when belief in God becomes difficult, the natural tendency is to turn away from Him, but for heaven's sake, to what? If you did not find the answers you were looking for before you came to Christ, how can you find them by leaving Him and going back to where you were before?

Non-stop prayer

Prayer can be exhausting when we don't see an end to it.

Hope deferred maketh the heart sick: but when the desire cometh, it is a tree of life. Proverbs 13:12

Have you ever felt heartsick because of waiting and waiting for a situation to be resolved? I know I have.

One good thing that happened in my own life while waiting on God for many years was the development of non-stop prayer. Previously, I had never understood the scripture, *"Pray without ceasing."* (1 Thessalonians 5:17)

How can a person pray without ceasing? Well, I learned how. I learned that I am utterly helpless without God. I learned that any abilities that I think I might have, or any strengths that I think I may possess, all come from Him. All He would have to do is withhold them, and there would be nothing left of my so-called abilities or strengths.

The prayers I pray are probably pretty comical to the average person, which is why I usually pray silently.

Dear Lord, please help me walk into the building without tripping.

Please remind me to buy cat food.

Oh God, help me remember to signal my turns!

You may laugh, but I have learned that when I forget to pray about these trivial matters, I trip, my cat has no food, and I get pulled over by a police officer. God is so faithful. If He answers the smallest, most inconsequential prayers (and I assure you, He does), He will certainly attend to the biggest and most important matters.

Prayer is absolutely essential to the Christian life. If you can't pray an impressive, flowery prayer (which does nothing to impress God, anyway) just cry out to Him. Sometimes my prayers consist of only three words, repeated over and over as my tears stream down: "Lord, have mercy."

Satan loves nothing more than to destroy our prayer life. Since God commands us to do it, Satan fights against it. Let's fight back.

Chapter 5: Reading the Bible

Jesus Christ is The Word of God.

In the beginning was the Word, and the Word was with God, and the Word was God. The same was in the beginning with God. John 1:1-2

And the Word was made flesh, and dwelt among us (and we beheld his glory, the glory as of the only begotten of the Father), full of grace and truth. John 1:14

When we read the written word, the Bible, we are to store it in our hearts. We are to meditate on it, and bring it out now and then, when we need it. And trust me, we always need it.

Years ago, I was talking to a fellow believer who said that he used to read the Bible, but didn't anymore, because different people had contradictory things to say about it, and it just confused him, so he stopped.

Not to be rude, but what a lame excuse. If I want to become a nuclear physicist, I am going to have to read about nuclear physics. I am sure there are probably several different viewpoints or theories on nuclear physics. Should I give up reading about it, because of conflicting viewpoints? Or should I pursue the study of it, until I find the truth?

It depends on what I want. If I want to be a nuclear physicist, I'd better keep reading.

Is nuclear physics something that is so very easy to understand? No.

If something is worthwhile, it is almost never easy. And if something is easy, it is almost never worthwhile.

The Lord knows that you are spiritually exhausted. He is infinitely tender with His sheep. He will never drive you to collapse.

He shall feed his flock like a shepherd: he shall gather the lambs with his arm, and carry them in his bosom, and shall gently lead those that are with young. Isaiah 40:11

Is it possible, dear saint, that you are exhausted because you are "with young?" Are you spiritually pregnant, and about to give birth to something new in His kingdom?

When a woman is pregnant in the natural realm, she tires more easily. She moves more slowly. She requires more rest. Carrying a child is physically taxing, even though the mother-to-be is not at all actively involved in the assembling of her baby. She does not wake up in the morning and say, "Today I am going to work on the eyes, tomorrow I will work on the toes, and the day after that I will make sure the hair is growing." No, thankfully, blissfully, she does not have that responsibility. She simply provides a safe environment for the child to grow, and makes sure that it has enough nutritious food. God does the rest.

When you are spiritually pregnant, you tire more easily. You move more slowly. You require more rest.

God knows what you are carrying. He will gently lead you. Just be willing to be led by Him. He will do the rest.

Read your Bible every day. It doesn't matter how many times you have read it; the Lord will show you something new each day. It will be something that you need to hear at that time. It is your daily bread.

Those of us who live in the West have the enormous privilege of having Bibles to read. Let's not take that privilege for granted. Remember that in Muslim-controlled countries, possession of a Bible means imprisonment or death. Read your Bible, and thank God for it.

Memorize His word. I like to write verses down on index cards. I keep some on my refrigerator, and some on my desk at work. It is not always practical to carry a physical Bible with you everywhere you go, but if you have hidden His word in your heart, you definitely can carry it with you! Of course, if you're a part of the younger generation of Christians, you have your Bible on your phone, which you carry everywhere you go.

When we are spiritually exhausted, reading the Bible becomes hard, just like everything else becomes hard. When you simply can't absorb Leviticus, turn to the Psalms instead.

Thy word have I hid in mine heart, that I might not sin against thee. Psalm 119:11

Thy word is a lamp unto my feet, and a light unto my path. Psalm 119:105

How precious also are thy thoughts unto me, O God! how great is the sum of them! Psalm 139:17

I have found the Psalms to be very renewing to my spirit. In-depth Bible study is very important, Hebrew and Greek dictionaries and all, but sometimes our weary souls just need the beautiful, restoring melodies of the Psalms. Even today, many of the Psalms have been put to music and are sung in our churches. You can read them over and over again, and let the Holy Spirit minister to your soul.

When we are spiritually exhausted because of sin (see chapter 8), Psalm 51 is especially helpful.

Create in me a clean heart, O God; and renew a right spirit within me. Cast me not away from thy presence; and take not thy holy spirit from me. Restore unto me the joy of thy salvation; and uphold me with thy free spirit. Psalm 51:10-12

Amen.

Chapter 6: Doing good works

And let us consider one another to provoke unto love and to good works... Hebrews 10:24

I am in our church's building. It is Friday afternoon, and I am the only one there.

I start in the bathrooms - sweeping the floors and flinging the dust out. I scrub the toilets and the sinks. I refill the soap dispensers and clean the mirrors. Moving to the tiny kitchen, I put away the clean dishes, wash the dirty dishes, and wipe off the counters. What's this? Stale food in the fridge, left over from our last church dinner. I toss it.

Retrieving the vacuum from the closet, I vacuum up the dust I flung onto the carpet earlier. I put offering envelopes in the backs of the seat pockets. I wipe off the glass tables at the front.

Are the microphone stands set up? What about the offering basket? Is there a tissue box and water bottle at the pulpit?

I stand near the front, surveying all.

Sunday is "game on," and everything has to be perfect, or as near perfect as things can be in this fallen human realm. Our pastors carry such a huge burden; the last thing they need to worry about is whether there is toilet paper in the bathrooms.

I look around one last time. I think everything is okay. I whisper a final prayer, turn off all the lights, gather up the big sack of garbage, and head out the door.

Years before, I had asked our pastor for a key to the building. I wanted to come in and clean once a week, I told him. I was surprised and rather taken aback when I was told no. Later, I heard the rest of the story.

Our pastor is a very generous and unselfish person. Over the years he had let several people have keys to the building. Many a Sunday morning he had arrived early for service, only to find fast food bags on the floor of the sanctuary, crumbs on the carpet, chairs in disarray, and all the lights on. Some people who had been given the privilege of a key to the church building had decided to use it as their own personal hang-out with friends.

Needless to say, I was horrified when I learned of this. I was also quite indignant. How could people do that? What disrespect!

I explained to the pastor that my only reason for asking for a key was so that I could clean the building, period. I have no friends to eat fast food with, anyway (not true, but I think he understood what I meant), and when I want to "hang out," I want to do it at a coffee shop, not in the church sanctuary. After several months, during which time I believe he was observing my behavior, he allowed me to have a key. By this time, we were about to transition to a different building with a new set of locks, and the fast-food bandits had all drifted away from the church.

So, I took my key ownership very seriously. I took my cleaning duties very seriously – I admit, sometimes too seriously. At times I was a "sanctuary Nazi," coming down very hard on the young people with their bags of chips. "Take that back to the kitchen!" I would bark at them.

One day, in despair, I remarked to one of the young ladies, "When I was growing up, it was absolutely unheard of to bring food into church, unless it was a potluck dinner, of course. No one did it; it would be like lighting up a cigarette in the sanctuary."

She stared at me in disbelief. "In the Sudanese church, everyone brings food in, all the time," she said.

I had to bite my tongue to keep from saying, "Well, this ain't Sudan!" Thankfully, I kept my mouth shut.

Cleaning our church building is one very small thing I can do to help our pastors. They pray for us, night and day. They fast and intercede when someone in the congregation is in distress. Going without food and sleep is a normal routine for them. I remember all this when I wonder why I'm there once again, cleaning. Oh yeah, I volunteered!

The Bible tells us that God Himself created good works for us to do, before He created us! That is mind-boggling to me.

For we are his workmanship, created in Christ Jesus unto good works, which God hath before ordained that we should walk in them. Ephesians 2:10

The Bible has a lot to say about good works. Many of us were raised on the "grace alone" doctrine, so it's helpful to be reminded of what God thinks about our good works.

Let your light so shine before men, that they may see your good works, and glorify your Father which is in heaven. Matthew 5:16

In all things shewing thyself a pattern of good works: in doctrine shewing uncorruptness, gravity, sincerity... Titus 2:7

One of the ways that unbelievers see that you and I love Jesus is by the good things that we do.

Having your conversation honest among the Gentiles: that, whereas they speak against you as evildoers, they may by your good works, which they shall behold, glorify God in the day of visitation. 1 Peter 2:12

When I am having a hard day at work, I just want to go home. The last thing I want to do is take on more work. But when I see a co-worker struggling, and I offer to help her, an amazing thing happens. My exhaustion is lifted, and she sees Jesus in me.

This is a faithful saying, and these things I will that thou affirm constantly, that they which have believed in God might be careful to maintain good works. These things are good and profitable unto men. Titus 3:8

Christians seem to swing from one extreme to another. Some groups emphasize good works and don't bother to mention salvation, or worse, preach that salvation comes by good works. Other groups seem to frown on good works, because, if you're saved by grace alone, what's the point of doing good works?

It's easy to think that you have reached some sort of high, mystical, spiritual plane where you are far above the realm of doing any kind of work on this planet. Good works seem to belong to the lower realm, where all the mere mortals live. But when the glory clouds have lifted, someone still needs to take out the trash.

Jesus did a very basic good work when He fed a huge crowd of people by multiplying bread and fish. I can't supernaturally multiply food (yet – John 14:12), but perhaps I can pay for the food for a church conference. People who are coming to hear the word of God need to eat, and they need a place to stay, and their dirty dishes need to be washed. I can do all of that.

Like anything else we do as a part of our Christian faith, we can become exhausted doing good works. For me, it is more of a mental than a physical exhaustion. The devil loves to remind me, as I am exiting the building with the bag of trash, that what I am doing doesn't matter, that it is a tiny drop in the bucket of everything that needs to be done, and that I didn't do a good enough job of it, anyway.

The Lord knows that we have a tendency to get exhausted while doing good works. That's why He warned us:

And let us not be weary in well doing: for in due season we shall reap, if we faint not. Galatians 6:9

When will this "due season" come, I wonder?

But he that shall endure unto the end, the same shall be saved. Matthew 24:13

God warned Cain that he needed to do the right thing. He didn't tell Cain that everything in his life would be fine, and that what Cain did or didn't do didn't really matter, because, after all, God is grace and mercy. No. He said:

If thou doest well, shalt thou not be accepted? and if thou doest not well, sin lieth at the door. Genesis 4:7a

It is very sobering to think that if I do not do the right thing, sin is crouching at my door, waiting to pounce on me.

Yes, God forgives us when we sin, and I thank Him for it every day. But He also expects us to do the right thing!

...refuse the evil, and choose the good. Isaiah 7:15b

When I stand before Him on judgement day, this is what I want to happen:

His lord said unto him, Well done, good and faithful servant; thou hast been faithful over a few things, I will make thee ruler over many things: enter thou into the joy of thy lord. Matthew 25:23

Chapter 7: The wrong place at the wrong time

Many years ago, I was asked to teach children's Sunday school. The church I was a part of at that time was in need of a children's teacher, and I seemed to be the most logical choice. People who are willing to work in children's ministry always seem to be in short supply. I knew this, so I said yes, even though I knew in my heart I was not gifted in that area.

The first Sunday that I taught, there were eleven children, including my own son. The second Sunday, there were four children, including my son. The third Sunday, my son and I sat across a table from each other in that otherwise empty room, and he was perplexed.

"How come none of the other kids came, Mom?" he asked. I gave him some excuse that I don't remember today. I knew why they had not come!

Thankfully, my short-lived foray into children's ministry did not result in spiritual exhaustion. But had I continued in that area, it would have most certainly happened.

You can't fit a square peg into a round hole. If you find yourself constantly exhausted in your spiritual life, it is a guarantee that you are ministering in the wrong area.

Bear in mind that there is a difference between being tired from ministering, and spiritual exhaustion. Jesus often went off by Himself, to be alone with God and pray. He needed to refresh and renew Himself before ministering again. This is very necessary.

When Jesus heard of it, he departed thence by ship into a desert place apart... Matthew 14:13a

And when he had sent the multitudes away, he went up into a mountain apart to pray: and when the evening was come, he was there alone. Matthew 14:23

Then cometh Jesus with them unto a place called Gethsemane, and saith unto the disciples, Sit ye here, while I go and pray yonder. Matthew 26:36

When you are doing what God has called you to do, you will feel energized, not exhausted. This doesn't mean that you won't need to occasionally rest – you will. But after you rest, you will return to your duties with renewed zeal and joy.

Sometimes, when we are in the wrong position, we can deceive ourselves that we are in the right position. When a person is under that deception, it is not necessarily he that becomes exhausted, but everyone around him does.

We read in 1 Samuel 1 – 3 the story of Eli the priest, and his two sons, Hophni and Phinehas. The Bible doesn't go into great detail about Eli and whether he was at one time a true man of God. We do read, however, that near the end of his life, he placed other things above God.

Now Eli was very old, and heard all that his sons did unto all Israel; and how they lay with the women that assembled at the door of the tabernacle of the congregation. And he said unto them, Why do ye such things? for I hear of your evil dealings by all this people. Nay, my sons; for it is no good report that I hear: ye make the LORD's people to transgress. If one man sin against another, the judge shall judge him: but if a man sin against the LORD, who shall intreat for him? Notwithstanding they hearkened not unto the voice of their father, because the LORD would slay them. 1 Samuel 2:22 - 25

Another man of God came to Eli and warned him what would happen, if he didn't correct his sons.

And this shall be a sign unto thee, that shall come upon thy two sons, on Hophni and Phinehas; in one day they shall die both of them. 1 Samuel 2:34

Earlier we read a blistering description of Eli's sons, and what they were doing.

Now the sons of Eli were sons of Belial; they knew not the LORD. And the priest's custom with the people was, that, when any man offered sacrifice, the priest's servant came, while the flesh was in seething, with a fleshhook of three teeth in his hand; And he struck it into the pan, or kettle, or caldron, or pot; all that the fleshhook brought up the priest took for himself. So they did in Shiloh unto all the Israelites that came thither. Also before they burnt the fat, the priest's servant came, and said to the man that sacrificed, Give flesh to roast for the priest; for he will not have sodden flesh of thee, but raw. And if any man said unto him, Let them not fail to burn the fat presently, and then take as much as thy soul desireth; then he would answer him, Nay; but thou shalt give it me now: and if not, I will take it by force. Wherefore the sin of the young men was very great before the LORD: for men abhorred the offering of the LORD. 1 Samuel 2:12 - 17

The Jews were commanded to offer the very best to the Lord in their sacrifices. The Lord took what He wanted from the burnt offering, and the priest took what was left over, not the other way around!
Imagine how you would feel if you brought an animal to the temple, to be sacrificed to the Lord, and the priest kept the best part of the animal for himself, and said that whatever was left over would go to the Lord. You would not be happy!

34

And if this happened time and again, you would begin to wonder why you were bothering to bring sacrifices in the first place. The sacrifices were supposed to be for the Lord, yet a selfish and wicked man took them for himself. You may, under these circumstances, stop bringing sacrifices altogether. What would be the point?

God does not take these things lightly.

Ye offer polluted bread upon mine altar; and ye say, Wherein have we polluted thee? In that ye say, The table of the LORD is contemptible. And if ye offer the blind for sacrifice, is it not evil? and if ye offer the lame and sick, is it not evil? offer it now unto thy governor; will he be pleased with thee, or accept thy person? saith the LORD of hosts. Malachi 1:7-8

Whether we like it or not, someone is always watching us. If I give my leftovers to God, whether it's time, money, service, devotion, or whatever it may be, be assured that God knows this, and someone else, or many other people, are also influenced by what I am doing.

Nay, my sons; for it is no good report that I hear: ye make the LORD's people to transgress. 1 Samuel 2:24

But whoso shall offend one of these little ones which believe in me, it were better for him that a millstone were hanged about his neck, and that he were drowned in the depth of the sea. Matthew 18:6

If you or I are in the wrong position, doing the wrong thing, we can cause others to stumble. This simply means that we can cause others to turn away from God, or to sin, or to move into a wrong position also.

Too many people turn away from the Lord because of something someone in the church did. Sometimes these people try to correct the situation by confronting the person who was doing wrong, but too often, the matter does not get resolved properly, and the person who was wronged becomes exhausted from dealing with the situation, and leaves the church. When I say "leaves the church," I don't mean they start fellowshipping somewhere else. I mean they turn their backs on God and Christianity in general.

I don't want to be responsible for that!

No, I can't do everything perfectly all the time. And, I should not be overly concerned about what people think of me. That in itself always leads to spiritual exhaustion. But if you are not sure if something is pleasing to the Lord, ask yourself this question: How would I feel if I saw one of the young people in the church doing or saying what I am thinking about doing or saying? If you feel uncomfortable at the thought of someone else doing it, you probably shouldn't do it.

The danger always arises that legalism will creep in. Legalism will effectively kill a local church. Legalism adds a whole bunch of rules and regulations to our behavior that God Himself never added, nor requires of us.

If you are one of those people who likes to follow the rules, you will have a natural tendency to notice when others aren't following the rules, and you will want to correct them. Just as I did with the young people and their bags of chips!

While correction is sometimes necessary, it is imperative that you examine your own heart before correcting someone. In the church I grew up in, I was chastised for wearing pants, wearing a sleeveless shirt, wearing heels that were too high, and wearing makeup. These corrections all came from people who truly loved God and wanted to please Him, but unfortunately, these people were very legalistic.

For they bind heavy burdens and grievous to be borne, and lay them on men's shoulders; but they themselves will not move them with one of their fingers. Matthew 23:4

Young people, especially, can become spiritually exhausted by following an extra set of rules that their church expects them to follow, yet which are not laid out in the Bible. Sometimes the results of this are downright comical.

A friend of mine told me this story. A young woman began attending her church. Everyone noticed the newcomer, because each Sunday she wore a micro-mini skirt, extremely low-cut shirt, and stiletto heels. My friend, who is one of the kindest people I have ever met, finally took this woman aside and invited her, in private, to go shopping with her. The woman hesitated, and finally told my friend that she was really short on cash. My supernaturally kind friend told her not to worry about it; she would foot the bill.

So, they went shopping, and my friend picked out some very nice and modest skirts and tops for the young woman to wear. In the course of their shopping expedition, the woman revealed to my friend that she had wanted to come to church for some time, but had heard that skirts are "required" in church, and the only skirts she owned were those that she wore when going to the nightclub. So, that's what she had worn to church.

What a tragic/comic situation! What if this woman had decided to wear a simple pair of khakis and a regular sweater to church, similar to what a lot of us wear in the workplace? Few people would have noticed. But since she'd heard that skirts were required, she made do with what she had. After all, you can't go to church wearing pants! That's illegal, isn't it?

My friend handled the situation with the newcomer exactly right, in my opinion. She had a private conversation with her, helped her correct the problem, and even used her own money to correct it. The newcomer was not humiliated or made to feel ashamed or "less than." The rest of the congregation would no longer feel uncomfortable by her presence, and everyone came out on top. It was truly a win-win for all.

Legalism can result in many strange situations. A group I know does not allow any work to be done on the sabbath day. Yet, they allow shopping on the sabbath day. That one left me scratching my head. Is not schlepping all those heavy bags from the car into the house considered work? Apparently not.

What makes this even more tragic is that when a person finally breaks free from a legalistic system, he or she often swings very far to the opposite extreme. Another friend of mine was telling me that smoking and drinking alcohol are forbidden in her church. Invariably, when people leave the church, they start smoking and drinking. That seems painfully ridiculous to me. Regardless of whether your church "allows" smoking and drinking, why on earth would you want to destroy your own body, just to get back at them?

My mother used to have a saying: "Don't cut off your nose to spite your face."

I wonder if Hophni and Phineas were an example of those who had swung to the opposite extreme. Perhaps they had seen firsthand the mercy and grace of God, and experienced

His forgiveness personally. Maybe they thought that since God is so merciful and forgiving, He wouldn't mind if they slept with the women who served in the temple, or kept the best part of the sacrificial animals for themselves.

We can't know for sure, because the Bible doesn't tell us. But we do know that God really did mind.

And the messenger answered and said, Israel is fled before the Philistines, and there hath been also a great slaughter among the people, and thy two sons also, Hophni and Phinehas, are dead, and the ark of God is taken. And it came to pass, when he made mention of the ark of God, that (Eli) fell from off the seat backward by the side of the gate, and his neck brake, and he died: for he was an old man, and heavy. And he had judged Israel forty years. 1 Samuel 17 – 18

What a price to pay for being in the wrong place at the wrong time. Hophni and Phineas paid with their lives, and Eli paid with his life, because he had the authority and the ability to correct his sons' behavior, and he didn't do it.

Chapter 8: Sin

Nothing is quite as exhausting as sin.

The sin of depression

There is no soundness in my flesh because of thine anger; neither is there any rest in my bones because of my sin. For mine iniquities are gone over mine head: as an heavy burden they are too heavy for me. Psalm 38: 3 - 4

When we are living a life of sin, we are carrying a heavy burden indeed.   Living a life of sin doesn't describe only those who are living as drug addicts, prostitutes or murderers. Many Bible-believing Christians are living a life of habitual sin. Some are aware of it, but many aren't.

I came face to face with this in my own life. Like Elijah, I suffered from bouts of depression that were crippling.

But he himself went a day's journey into the wilderness, and came and sat down under a juniper tree: and he requested for himself that he might die; and said, It is enough; now, O LORD, take away my life; for I am not better than my fathers. 1 Kings 19:4

Depression is a sin. I realize this is a sensitive subject for many people, but it is a fact, nevertheless. When we are depressed, we are in effect telling God that He is not enough for us, and that He needs to do a better job of arranging our lives.

Satan is very clever. He usually arranges depression to hit us after we have had a tremendous victory in some area.

Elijah called down fire from heaven and killed the false prophets of Baal. Right after that, he fled into the wilderness because Jezebel threatened to kill him, and he asked the Lord to take his life.

Meriwether Lewis, one-half of the famous explorer team of Lewis and Clark of the early nineteenth century, fell into a deep depression after the team's successful completion of the "Corp of Discovery" and their return to their former lives. History records his death as a possible suicide.

Buzz Aldrin, one of the very few people to ever walk on the moon, experienced severe depression after returning to Earth. "I wanted to resume my duties, but there were no duties to resume," he wrote in *Magnificent Desolation*. "There was no goal, no sense of calling, no project worth pouring myself into."

Someone once asked Elvis Presley to describe himself in one word. He said, "Alone."

After you have done what few other people have ever done, you are on top of the world. You feel exultant, high, empowered, and almost super-human. But it doesn't take long before you realize that you are not super-human; you are simply human.

Famous explorers, astronauts and performers are used to receiving kudos from their fans. Some come to expect this and develop an over-inflated ego. Others believe that the praise they are receiving is unmerited, and they feel that they have to do better, do more, perform better, and come up with more magnificent ideas, until they simply burn out from exhaustion. This leads to deep depression.

I am troubled; I am bowed down greatly; I go mourning all the day long. Psalm 38:6

After one of my books won a national award, I was so happy that I don't think my feet touched the ground for a week. I went around smiling at everyone, even strangers. If they frowned in return, I just smiled all the more. I felt as though my head was in the clouds and I was far above every earthly problem. But in the back of my mind, there was a nagging feeling. I knew that God had allowed me to win this award, and I also knew that Satan was aware of it. I began to wonder what Satan was going to do to bring me down. He has an ancient playbook that he uses, and his methods never vary. Because the Lord was gracious to me and showed me what was coming, I began to pray against the spirit of depression, which I knew from past experience Satan would try to attack me with. By God's grace, I escaped it.

It is important to overcome depression, just as it is important to overcome every other sin in our lives.

After Elijah fled from Jezebel, an angel came and ministered to him by bringing him food and water (1 Kings 19:5 - 8). The Lord certainly knew that Elijah was at the end of his rope, and he knows when you and I are, too. I can remember at one time in my life being so depressed that I couldn't even go to the grocery store. I thank God for His saints who came alongside me and lifted me up. Many times, I would find bags of groceries on my doorstep. I thank God to this day for those people and their kindness to me.

After Elijah received the supernatural food that the angel left for him, he went on a long journey. He was still running away. God, who sees all and knows all, knew that Elijah was running, but He asked him about it anyway.

42

*And he (Elijah) came thither unto a cave, and lodged there; and, behold, the word of the LORD came to him, and he said unto him, What doest thou here, Elijah? And he said, I have been very jealous for the LORD God of hosts: for the children of Israel have forsaken thy covenant, thrown down thine altars, and slain thy prophets with the sword; and I, even I only, am left; and they seek my life, to take it away. And he said, Go forth, and stand upon the mount before the LORD. And, behold, the LORD passed by, and a great and strong wind rent the mountains, and brake in pieces the rocks before the LORD; but the LORD was not in the wind: and after the wind an earthquake; but the LORD was not in the earthquake: And after the earthquake a fire; but the LORD was not in the fire: and after the fire a still small voice. And it was so, when Elijah heard it, that he wrapped his face in his mantle, and went out, and stood in the entering in of the cave. And, behold, there came a voice unto him, and said, What doest thou here, Elijah? And he said, I have been very jealous for the LORD God of hosts: because the children of Israel have forsaken thy covenant, thrown down thine altars, and slain thy prophets with the sword; and I, even I only, am left; and they seek my life, to take it away. And the LORD said unto him, Go, return on thy way to the wilderness of Damascus…*1 Kings 19:9 – 15

It's interesting that God asked Elijah twice what he was doing hiding in a cave, and twice Elijah gave God the same reply. To put it in modern day language, Elijah was telling God, "Lord, You don't understand. I've worked for You so zealously. Your people, Israel, are a bunch of idolaters. They kill anyone who tries to tell them the truth. I'm the only one left who is serving You, and now they're trying to kill me, too." Elijah repeated this twice, to make sure that God heard it.

On the surface, God didn't seem to have much sympathy for Elijah. It was as though He didn't hear him. He just gave him a list of instructions, told him where to go and what to do, and told him what would happen after he did it (1 Kings 19:15-17). Then, almost as an afterthought, God told Elijah something that he really needed to hear.

Yet I have left me seven thousand in Israel, all the knees which have not bowed unto Baal, and every mouth which hath not kissed him. 1 Kings 19:18

That is the key. When you are overwhelmed by depression, you believe you are all alone. You believe you are the only one who is going through what you're going through. But you're not. Elijah believed he was the only person left who loved God and was serving Him. I think he was more than a little surprised to learn that there were seven thousand other people who loved God, in addition to him.

One of the best cures for depression is to try to help someone else who needs help. Once Elijah got clear direction from God, he stopped hiding in the cave and set out to anoint the kings, as God had instructed him. If you have clear instructions from God, by all means, carry them out. If you don't, reach out to someone else and help that person. In my own case, I began giving money and food to homeless people that I saw on the street. Even though my rational mind argued that I didn't have enough money to be handing it out (and I really didn't), I made a great effort to do it anyway. I, at least, had a roof over my head. God always blesses me when I do this, and it always lifts my spirits.

You can volunteer at a homeless shelter, battered women's shelter, children's hospital, or assisted living center. I guarantee you, you will feel better.

There is nothing wrong with the *feeling* of depression. We all feel it from time to time.

And when he (Jesus) was come near, he beheld the city, and wept over it, Saying, If thou hadst known, even thou, at least in this thy day, the things which belong unto thy peace! but now they are hid from thine eyes. For the days shall come upon thee, that thine enemies shall cast a trench about thee, and compass thee round, and keep thee in on every side, And shall lay thee even with the ground, and thy children within thee; and they shall not leave in thee one stone upon another; because thou knewest not the time of thy visitation. Luke 19:41 – 45

O Jerusalem, Jerusalem, thou that killest the prophets, and stonest them which are sent unto thee, how often would I have gathered thy children together, even as a hen gathereth her chickens under her wings, and ye would not! Matthew 23:37

Jesus wept over Jerusalem, because He knew what was about to happen to it. If Jesus can weep, so can we.

We need to cry out to God and be very honest with Him regarding our circumstances. He knows, anyway.

I cried unto the LORD with my voice; with my voice unto the LORD did I make my supplication. I poured out my complaint before him; I shewed before him my trouble. When my spirit was overwhelmed within me, then thou knewest my path. In the way wherein I walked have they privily laid a snare for me. Psalm 142:1 - 3

After you have cried out to God, start moving. When a person is deeply depressed, even getting out of bed in the morning seems impossible. But put one foot in front of the other, and start moving, no matter how slowly. Find that person who needs help. Your spirits will lift.

Depression becomes a sin when we remain mired in it. Lest anyone think I am criticizing, I will tell you that I am an expert in this area, because I allowed myself to become mired in depression. With the help of my pastors, a mighty man and woman of God, I realized that God had a purpose for my life, even though at the time I couldn't imagine what it was, and if I would step out in faith, He would give me tasks to do that would give me a reason to get out of bed every morning. And He did.

Carrying the heavy sin burden of depression will make you spiritually exhausted. Give it to Jesus instead.

The sin of worry

Many Christians live a life of constant worry. This is also a sin. And guess what? Constant worry often leads to depression.

Take therefore no thought for the morrow: for the morrow shall take thought for the things of itself. Sufficient unto the day is the evil thereof. Matthew 6:34

Too many people spend way too much time worrying about things that never happen. This is another area in which I am an expert!

And take heed to yourselves, lest at any time your hearts be overcharged with surfeiting, and drunkenness, and cares of this life, and so that day come upon you unawares. Luke 21:34

In the verse above, Jesus was warning His followers that when He returns, many people will be caught off guard. One reason given for this is that people's hearts will be overwhelmed with cares (worry).

Worrying has been compared to being in a rocking chair. You go back and forth, but you never get anywhere. As an expert worrier, I have worried about not having enough money to pay my bills, and not making it to where I need to be on time. I have worried about disappointing those who are counting on me, and getting into a car accident. I have worried about my son and his friends. I have worried about getting old. And, I have worried about many things that are too private to list here!

One thing that all these worries have in common: there is very, very little that I can do to change any of them. So why worry? And yet we all do, from time to time.

The scripture does not record anywhere that Jesus ever worried. I don't believe He did. He had full and complete trust in God to do whatever was best in His life, so He had nothing to worry about. Let's follow His example.

The sin of jealousy

Being jealous of another person will certainly lead to exhaustion.

For we dare not make ourselves of the number, or compare ourselves with some that commend themselves: but they measuring themselves by themselves, and comparing them-selves among themselves, are not wise.
2 Corinthians 10:12

Comparing yourself to another person will result in one of two things: pride or depression. You will always find someone that you think is better than you are. And, you will always find someone that you think you are better than. Both beliefs are false.

Then Peter opened his mouth, and said, Of a truth I perceive that God is no respecter of persons... Acts 10:34

God loves each one of us and gives each one of us gifts, according to His will. He is the best giver. I may wish that I had other gifts or attributes, different than the ones He has given me, but His choice is always best.

All of my life I have been so envious of people who can write music. I have always wanted to do that, but I simply am not gifted in that area. I was amazed when someone told me that she was envious of me, because I could write poetry, and she couldn't. I had to repent of my jealousy of the music writers, and thank God for the poetic gift He's given me. And, who knows? Maybe someday some famous musician will set one of my poems to music!

Stop comparing yourself to other people. You don't know what they are going through. The thing that you are so jealous of that they have, most likely comes with a lot of baggage that you are not willing to carry. Praise God and thank God for what He's given you.

The sin of fear

Fear is also exhausting. When you live in fear, you are saying that you don't trust God to take care of you. Like depression, worry, and jealousy, we all feel fear from time to time, but fear becomes sin when it becomes a lifestyle. I am always amazed when I hear people talking about their fears. People are afraid of heights, storms, spiders, and the dark, but mostly, they are afraid of other people.

When I think about the times that I have been afraid of people, I have to remember that no one has any power over me, to harm me in any way, unless God allows that to happen. Instead of just plunging blindly into situations where I might get hurt (physically or emotionally), I need to pray and ask God for His protection over me. One thing I have learned from my very godly pastors is to pray before making a phone call, pray before visiting someone, and pray before embarking on a new venture. I have seen firsthand how situations that should have turned ugly, never did, and how arguments that should have started, never happened, because I committed the situation to prayer beforehand.

Commit thy way unto the LORD; trust also in him; and he shall bring it to pass. Psalm 37:5

All sin is exhausting. Let's remember these wise words:

If we confess our sins, he is faithful and just to forgive us our sins, and to cleanse us from all unrighteousness. 1 John 1:9

Chapter 9: Rebellion

For rebellion is as the sin of witchcraft, and stubbornness is as iniquity and idolatry. Because thou hast rejected the word of the LORD, he hath also rejected thee from being king. 1 Samuel 15:23

Some people are in rebellion against God and they don't even know it. Others know full well what they are doing, and they don't care.

In the verse above from 1 Samuel, the prophet told King Saul that God had rejected him. You and I may not be kings or queens, but we can apply this verse to our lives. Fill in the end of the verse with your circumstances:

Because you have rejected the word of the Lord, He has also rejected you for that promotion.

Because you have rejected the word of the Lord, He has also rejected you for that marriage.

Because you have rejected the word of the Lord, He has also rejected you for that ministry. Or,

…that child.

…that money.

…that blessing.

People who live in rebellion are exhausted. They go from one plan to another, one program to another, one idea to another, trying to put their lives in order and live at peace. And they can't.

There is a way that seemeth right unto a man, but the end thereof are the ways of death. Proverbs 16:25

Having turned away from God in rebellion, many people feel that they can't turn back to Him and ask for help. This is just silly pride. God is the *only* One who can help you and me.

I will lift up mine eyes unto the hills, from whence cometh my help. My help cometh from the LORD, which made heaven and earth. Psalm 121:1-2

It is tragically comical to watch a person who once walked with God, who is now living his life in rebellion. The prodigal son lived in a pig pen, literally, and thought he was doing okay, until he finally came to his senses (Luke 15:11-32).

Imagine how exhausted this son had been, living in rebellion away from his father. Like all sins, rebellion starts out very sweet, but it ends up very bitter. This son thought he was on top of the world – living the high life, drinking, partying, spending money on anything and everything. I'm sure he thought he didn't need his father at all (ironic, since his father was the one who originally gave him the money that he was now wasting). He probably thought his father was a rigid, repressive old man who was standing in the way of all his fun. So he left. But when the money ran out, the fun also ran out, and the prodigal son was snapped back to reality. Suddenly having to work for a living, when he had been used to a life of ease, suddenly going hungry, when he had been used to an abundance of food....this boy became exhausted in a hurry.

God had to bring this prodigal son to a very low place before he finally saw himself and his actions in the light of the truth.

Rebellion is exhausting! You constantly have to justify what you're doing – to yourself and others. You can't reach out for help, because that would be admitting that you are wrong, and a person caught in rebellion doesn't want to admit he's wrong!

People who abuse drugs and alcohol are in rebellion against their own bodies, their parents, their families, their bosses, etc., and they always have a list of plausible reasons why their rebellion is okay. "I can handle it. I can quit any time I want to. I just do it recreationally." And, on and on.

Then when lust hath conceived, it bringeth forth sin: and sin, when it is finished, bringeth forth death. James 1:15

In the spiritual world and the natural world, one thing leads to another. In 1 Samuel 15, King Saul started out with one wrong desire (translated as lust in the King James Bible). He wanted to please the people, rather than please God. The wrong desire turned into one "little" sin – he disobeyed God (rebelled) by not killing all of the Amalekite people and all of their animals, as God had commanded him to do. He left the king of the Amalekites alive, and some of the best animals. When confronted with his sin, he made excuses and blamed others. His sin then turned into death – not his physical death, but the death of his kingdom.

Because thou hast rejected the word of the LORD, he hath also rejected thee from being king. 1 Samuel 15:23b

Jonah's story is another classic case of rebellion. The Lord told Jonah to go to Nineveh to preach to the people there. Jonah fled from God and sailed on a ship in the opposite direction. He rebelled against God because he didn't like the Ninevites and didn't want to preach to them. His rebellion caused a huge storm that threatened the lives of many other people. Because Jonah was a godly man, although rebellious, he realized that the storm was his fault, and told the captain to throw him overboard.

The Bible doesn't explicitly tell us this, but I think we can infer that Jonah believed he would die in the ocean. I'm sure he had no foreknowledge of the huge fish that God was sending to swallow him. Imagine being so exhausted from running away from God, that death seems to be your only option. Maybe Jonah thought that he had crossed a line when he ran away from God. Maybe the thought of death was a welcome idea to him.

After spending three days and nights in the fish's belly, the Lord told the fish to vomit Jonah up. He then found dry land and had to make his way to Nineveh. I'm sure he was many miles away, and his trip back was a lot longer and harder than it needed to be, because of his rebellion.

Rebellion causes delays in receiving God's blessings. If you or I are rebelling against God, we will not be in the right place at the right time to receive the blessings He wants to give us.

Too many churches are in rebellion against God. It seems shocking to put it that way, but it's the truth. Rebellion doesn't have to mean smoking and drinking, and running around with women (or men). Rebellion is simply defined as doing something other than what God wants you to do.

I will never forget a group I was a part of, many years ago. We would go out to the local prison and have Bible study and prayer with the prisoners. We followed a very rigid program – pray, sing, listen to a message, pray, and conclude. It never varied. Having grown up in a charismatic/Pentecostal church, I felt a little uncomfortable with such a rigid format, but since I wasn't the one in charge, I didn't feel like I could say much about it.

One day we had just arrived, and several of us were standing around talking. One of the prisoners said to the group leader, "I've been thinking about this all week, and I've decided that I want to give my life to Jesus Christ tonight." I was overjoyed, and wanted to run over to this man and pray with him to receive Christ, then and there.

The group leader, Terry (not his real name), smiled and said, "That's great! We are going to have our opening prayer, then we'll sing, then we will hear the message, then we will have our closing prayer, and after that I will visit with you one-on-one so you can receive Christ."

The expression on the prisoner's face was a mixture of shock, disbelief, confusion, and anger. I stood there with my mouth hanging open, then shuffled over to my seat. I silently endured the rest of the evening. After the closing prayer, Terry approached the prisoner. I was on the other side of the room, so I couldn't hear their conversation, but I did see the prisoner shake his head and walk away. I then approached the group leader.

"What happened?" I asked. "Did he receive Christ?"

Terry frowned at me. "No," he said abruptly.

I couldn't keep my mouth shut. "Why not?" I asked. "Was it because you made him wait so long?"

This particular group leader had never liked me, and I'm sorry to say, the feeling was mutual. He looked at me disdainfully.

"It's not my responsibility to make people receive Christ," he snapped at me. "That's up to the Holy Spirit."

At that point I came just a little bit unglued. I was almost shouting. "Terry! Why are we here? I thought we were here to witness to the prisoners and lead them to Christ! Are we here to have a program, or to help people go to heaven? What good does all of this do if we're not leading people to Christ? You are wasting their time and ours!" (I've never been known for my tact.)

Terry walked away, muttering under his breath. I was commenting loudly, using all of my breath! The evening ended with all of us leaving and going our separate ways.

Sadly, I think some of the people in the group didn't even know that something wrong had occurred. So many people are so used to rigid programs that the idea of deviating from the program by one iota, even to save someone's life, is not even thought of.

I heard a similar story on the Christian radio station I listen to. A very well-known preacher, who I will decline to name, told the story of a young man who came to his church, at the end of his rope and the end of his life. After living the homosexual lifestyle for years, he had been diagnosed with HIV and didn't have long to live. This young man came to this particular church, seeking salvation. After listening to many songs, many prayers, a long sermon, more songs and more prayers, finally an altar call was given, and he went forward and received Christ. Later, during a time of testimony at this church, he testified about how long he had been waiting in the back row, with tears streaming down his face, for someone to extend an invitation to receive Christ. He didn't know anything about Jesus, nothing about church protocol or the Bible – he only knew he needed a savior.

Question: If you were in church and someone sitting near you had tears streaming down his face, wouldn't you take a "stop everything" approach and try to help the person?

Unfortunately, for too many people in too many churches, the answer to that question is "no." Why? Because it would disrupt the program.

The prison ministry I had been a part of and this huge church in California had one thing in common: both were operating in rebellion.

Many people will object and say, "The Bible says: Let all things be done decently and in order" (1 Corinthians 14:40). I heard a wise man of God say that there are two kinds of disorder. There is a disorderly disorder, and there is an orderly disorder. Anything going on in your church or mine that is not God's plan, no matter how orderly the service is being conducted, is disorder. And, I might add, it is rebellion against God.

How many people go to church in desperate straits, knowing they are dying spiritually (or physically!), knowing they need their lives to change, desperately seeking help, but instead they find very orderly programs that leave no room for salvation?

This type of situation exhausts people who are sincerely seeking answers. After the terrorist attacks on September 11, 2001, the churches in the United States were standing-room only. People were scared and seeking peace. People wanted to know that God was there and that He would help them. Instead, they encountered endless rituals with no life-changing power. It didn't take long for the churches to empty out again.

Then when lust hath conceived, it bringeth forth sin: and sin, when it is finished, bringeth forth death. James 1:15

Death is the end result of rebellion (sin). Your physical body may or may not die as a result of sin, but you can be sure that many other things will die – your fellowship with God, your relationships with other people, your finances, your good health, etc. Many churches have died because they prefer programs over the leading of the Holy Spirit.

I don't want to belabor this point, but this is a huge problem today. The church has done a very poor job of rescuing the lost. If your church has a food giveaway program, a clothing giveaway program, a youth sports program, a Christian AA program, and who knows what other program, but doesn't lead people to Jesus Christ, your church is in rebellion and is a failure in God's eyes.

To this day, I think about that prisoner who wanted to receive Christ, and was rebuffed in the name of "following the program." I wonder what happened to him. Did he go back to his cell thinking that Christianity was a false religion, and Christians were a bunch of fake people? I pray that God in His mercy sent another Christian to him, someone who was willing to put aside his religious program and offer life to this spiritually dead man. Did that prisoner ever receive Christ? I hope so.

I know thy works, that thou hast a name that thou livest, and art dead. Revelation 3:1b

I would rather see one person come to Christ, than follow one hundred structured programs in the name of religion, which doesn't lead anyone to Christ. I would rather be a part of an energized, living church, instead of a spiritually exhausted dead church.

Wouldn't you?

Chapter 10: Guilty conscience

Have you ever suffered from a guilty conscience? The longer you are carrying the weight of guilt, the more spiritually exhausted you will become.

For I acknowledge my transgressions: and my sin is ever before me. Against thee, thee only, have I sinned, and done this evil in thy sight: that thou mightest be justified when thou speakest, and be clear when thou judgest. Psalm 51:3-4

For mine iniquities are gone over mine head: as an heavy burden they are too heavy for me. Psalm 38:4

We can read the very sad story of King David's descent into adultery and murder in 2 Samuel 11.

After these events, he was carrying a heavy load of guilt. The Bible doesn't tell us that he was consciously aware that what he had done was wrong, at least not until the prophet Nathan came and pointed it out to him. That is the problem with sin. When we sin, it is very easy to begin to justify our actions. We can always come up with a good excuse as to why we did what we did.

If you are a born-again believer, the Holy Spirit will convict you of your sin. You will feel uneasy, restless, agitated, jumpy, and fearful. You will begin looking over your shoulder. "Does anyone else know what I did? Are they talking about me?"

If you have sinned against another person, you will feel uncomfortable around him or her. You will want to avoid that person. This is very exhausting. Inevitably, you will run into him or her, with no place to hide, and you will wish the ground would open up and swallow you.

But sometimes, we ignore the conviction of the Holy Spirit. We convince ourselves that we are right, and everyone else is wrong. This is a very dangerous situation to be in.

*Now the Spirit speaketh expressly, that in the latter times some shall depart from the faith, giving heed to seducing spirits, and doctrines of devils; Speaking lies in hypocrisy; having their conscience seared with a hot iron...*1 Timothy 4:1-2

The more you resist the Holy Spirit, the more your conscience will become seared. This doesn't happen overnight! Little compromises here and there eventually add up to a very dead conscience.

I believe that's what happened to King David. I believe it started when his men went out to war, and he remained behind. *(I've fought enough battles; I deserve a break.)* He slept during the day, and got out of bed as the sun was setting. *(I'm tired; I've been working too hard.)* He watched Bathsheba bathing. *(Wow – she's really beautiful.)*

At any point along this timeline, David could have stopped and done the opposite of what he was doing. But I believe he was mentally justifying his actions. And once he started justifying himself, it all went quickly downhill.

Staring at a beautiful woman taking a bath was not enough; he committed adultery with her. Impregnating her was an unplanned side effect of the adultery, so he tried to cover that up. When that plan failed, he had her husband murdered.

I believe that after David brought Bathsheba into the palace and took her as his wife, the physical effects of his guilty conscience began making themselves known, even if he was not aware of his sin in his conscious mind.

For my loins are filled with a loathsome disease: and there is no soundness in my flesh. Psalm 38:7

But I, as a deaf man, heard not; and I was as a dumb man that openeth not his mouth. Thus I was as a man that heareth not, and in whose mouth are no reproofs. Psalm 38:13-14

If you have a guilty conscience, you will have headaches, stomachaches, high blood pressure, depression, anxiety, and many other physical ailments. It's interesting how many people say that after they have confessed their sins and asked for forgiveness, they feel physically lighter and freer than they felt before. That's because sin is a very heavy burden to carry.

Humble yourselves therefore under the mighty hand of God, that he may exalt you in due time: Casting all your care upon him; for he careth for you. 1 Peter 5:6-7

The reason why we need to cast our cares (burdens) on Jesus is because they are too heavy for us to carry!

For mine iniquities are gone over mine head: as an heavy burden they are too heavy for me. Psalm 38:4

But they are not too heavy for Him to carry.

In order to ask for forgiveness, you have to humble yourself. A person who believes in his heart that he has no sin is refusing to humble himself. He will continue carrying that heavy burden month after month and year after year, and even if his conscious mind never realizes that he needs forgiveness, his body will tell him that he does! This is a sure-fire path to spiritual exhaustion.

Many people in the church try to fill up their days with lots of good activities (see chapter 6), trying to keep busy so they don't have to deal with their guilty consciences. Or worse, they think that by doing all those good things, they can somehow ease their consciences. I suppose David thought that providing Bathsheba with a beautiful home in his palace could somehow make up for his murdering her husband. But it didn't.

But the thing that David had done displeased the LORD. 2 Samuel 11:27b

We need to start seeing things the way God sees them.

Deliver me from bloodguiltiness, O God, thou God of my salvation: and my tongue shall sing aloud of thy righteousness. Psalm 51:14

Chapter 11: False guilt

Some of us don't appropriate full forgiveness. God has forgiven us, but we can't forgive ourselves. By refusing to forgive ourselves, we are holding ourselves to a higher standard than God holds us.

If we confess our sins, he is faithful and just to forgive us our sins, and to cleanse us from all unrighteousness. 1 John 1:9

As far as the east is from the west, so far hath he removed our transgressions from us. Psalm 103:12

He will turn again, he will have compassion upon us; he will subdue our iniquities; and thou wilt cast all their sins into the depths of the sea. Micah 7:19

If you have confessed your sins and asked God to forgive you, be assured, He has. Any guilt you feel over forgiven sin is false guilt, and it needs to be dealt with.

False guilt is a sin - just like lying, cheating, stealing, gossiping, adultery and murder. It's bad enough to commit these sins and be forgiven; let's not add false guilt to the list of things we need forgiveness for.

Sometimes when we have asked a human being to forgive us, that person refuses. So, even though we have also asked God for forgiveness, we don't feel forgiven, and we carry the weight of false guilt.

And the Lord turned, and looked upon Peter. And Peter remembered the word of the Lord, how he had said unto him, Before the cock crow, thou shalt deny me thrice. And Peter went out, and wept bitterly. Luke 22:61-62

Peter had a lot to cry about. He had denied Jesus. He pretended that he didn't know Him, at a time when Jesus needed His friends the most. When the Lord looked at him, Peter wept bitterly.

The Bible doesn't explicitly tell us this, but after Peter's betrayal, we know at some point that Jesus forgave him. Perhaps while he was crying tears, he was also crying out to God for forgiveness. I believe he was. After Jesus' resurrection, the angel told the women at the tomb:

But go your way, tell his disciples and Peter that he goeth before you into Galilee: there shall ye see him, as he said unto you. Mark 16:7

This was Jesus' way of saying, "Peter, you are still My disciple! You are still a part of the group, even though you betrayed Me."

In reading between the lines of the scripture, it seems to me that Peter didn't feel forgiven.

There were together Simon Peter, and Thomas called Didymus, and Nathanael of Cana in Galilee, and the sons of Zebedee, and two other of his disciples. Simon Peter saith unto them, I go a fishing. They say unto him, We also go with thee. They went forth, and entered into a ship immediately; and that night they caught nothing. John 21:2-3

I think Peter had concluded that his days of being Jesus' disciple were over. He decided to go back to his original profession: fishing. Some of Jesus' other disciples went with him. The Bible says they caught nothing.

Early in the morning, they saw Jesus standing on the shore. They pulled their boat in and went to talk with Him. He had made them breakfast, so they ate with Him.

So when they had dined, Jesus saith to Simon Peter, Simon, son of Jonas, lovest thou me more than these? He saith unto him, Yea, Lord; thou knowest that I love thee. He saith unto him, Feed my lambs. He saith to him again the second time, Simon, son of Jonas, lovest thou me? He saith unto him, Yea, Lord; thou knowest that I love thee. He saith unto him, Feed my sheep. He saith unto him the third time, Simon, son of Jonas, lovest thou me? Peter was grieved because he said unto him the third time, Lovest thou me? And he said unto him, Lord, thou knowest all things; thou knowest that I love thee. Jesus saith unto him, Feed my sheep. John 21:15-17

Putting myself in Peter's shoes, I think Peter was embarrassed that Jesus asked him three times whether he loved Him. I'm sure he was remembering that he had denied the Lord three times. He may have been thinking, "Why is He asking me this? I've denied Him, and He knows I denied Him. I do love Him, but I don't deserve His love in return."

Peter had to come to terms with the same concept that we all have to come to terms with. We don't deserve God's love. We don't deserve God's forgiveness.

This is what makes Christianity the most unique and most beautiful of all religious faiths. All other faiths, without exception, involve working your way to the top, so to speak. That is a concept that could only be conceived in the tiny mind of man. Think about it: God, who is perfect, completely holy, and without flaw, will somehow accept you if you do enough external good deeds. Since God doesn't tell you how many good deeds you have to do to be accepted by Him, you are forced to come up with a number in your own mind. If by some miracle you were able to do "enough" good deeds to become holy in God's eyes, you would no longer be human, because every human being has flaws, and no one is holy.

As it is written, There is none righteous, no, not one…
Romans 3:10

You would work your way into becoming God, which of course, is impossible.

Yet people keep trying to do this. Peter probably thought, "Jesus can't forgive me for denying Him. Somehow I've got to earn back His love and trust." Making the decision to go back to fishing probably meant he was at the end of his rope. "I've denied the Lord. There's no sense in continuing to preach His word. I'll go back to fishing."

Thankfully, the Lord appeared to Peter and the other disciples and gave them a little lesson about love. Jesus is perfect love and perfect forgiveness. When He forgives, He forgives completely. There was no longer any stain on Peter's record; everything had been washed clean. There was no longer any reason for him to carry false guilt for a sin that the Lord had forgiven.

False guilt sometimes comes from within our own soul, but it can also come from other people. The Bible tells us nothing about the other disciples' attitude toward Peter, but I wonder if some of them looked at him sideways after he denied Christ.

"I heard Peter say that he didn't know Jesus. He said it three times! True, I ran away when the soldiers came to get Jesus, but at least I didn't deny Him."

"Why is Jesus wasting His time asking Peter if he loves Him? If I was Him, I wouldn't even talk to Peter."

If this was in fact going on, and that is pure conjecture on my part, it would certainly add to Peter's load of false guilt. Sometimes we do our very best to forget the past, but other people are only too happy to remind us of it. Worse yet, they make up things that never happened and remind us of those!

I remember an occasion when someone I know started dredging up a load of incidents from years ago, and flinging them into my face. I listened, very puzzled, because none of the things he was talking about had actually happened. This person was doing his best to take me down, and since he had no live ammunition, he resorted to blanks. I think he finally realized that it wasn't working, probably due to the look of bewilderment on my face.

The devil is a liar, and everything he says is a lie. When you've confessed your sins and have been forgiven, it's a done deal. Close the book. God has.

Chapter 12: If only

And when Pharaoh drew nigh, the children of Israel lifted up their eyes, and, behold, the Egyptians marched after them; and they were sore afraid: and the children of Israel cried out unto the LORD. And they said unto Moses, Because there were no graves in Egypt, hast thou taken us away to die in the wilderness? wherefore hast thou dealt thus with us, to carry us forth out of Egypt? Is not this the word that we did tell thee in Egypt, saying, Let us alone, that we may serve the Egyptians? For it had been better for us to serve the Egyptians, than that we should die in the wilderness.
Exodus 14:10-12

It's hard to believe that someone would rather live a life of slavery instead of a life of freedom. The Israelites were rescued from slavery and were on their way to the promised land, when they saw Pharaoh's army approaching. Then they started saying, "If only…"

"If only we had stayed in Egypt! If only we hadn't listened to Moses! If only we had taken a different route! If only we had more weapons!"

When faced with what they thought was certain death, the Israelites started thinking that slavery was better. Slavery, as horrible as it is, at least is predictable.

Often, after we decide to go God's way, our lives get worse, not better. Then, we start longing for the past. When we were living in sin, we didn't have all these problems! (No, we just had a bunch of other problems.)

Sometimes we long for the past, because we want to re-do it.

"If only I hadn't said that. If only I hadn't been so insensitive. If only I wouldn't have done that. If only I would have listened."

I literally would have given my right arm to have re-done my past. If someone (with the legitimate ability to do this!) had told me that if I would cut off my right arm, I could go back in time and re-do my life, I would have found the nearest circular saw.

And if thy right hand offend thee, cut it off, and cast it from thee: for it is profitable for thee that one of thy members should perish, and not that thy whole body should be cast into hell. Matthew 5:30

This verse doesn't exactly apply to my situation, but the feeling behind it does apply. It's better to be physically maimed and spiritually whole, than to be physically whole and spiritually (or emotionally) maimed.

Until someone invents a time machine, none of us will be able to re-do our past. And unless we are careful, we will become spiritually exhausted by listening to all the "if onlys" that fill our minds.

Satan wants to keep you and me living in and agonizing over the past, because he knows there is not one thing we can do to change it. So, it may sound like a cliché, but concentrate on the things that you can change.

Awhile back, I was complaining inwardly about some things in my life that I did not like. Some of them I couldn't change, but some of them, I could! So I got started changing the things that I could. Some of these things were quite trivial, and some were more important. As I began taking steps to do things differently, I saw small changes for the better start to occur. This encouraged me, giving me the impetus to make a few more small changes.

It also gave me ammunition to use against the enemy. When he attacks my mind with "if only," I respond by reciting the positive changes I have made, and backing them up with scripture.

I can do all things through Christ which strengtheneth me. Philippians 4:13

Nay, in all these things we are more than conquerors through him that loved us. Romans 8:37

The devil is afraid of the word of God. Use the sword that God has given you – the word. That sends him scurrying out the door.

Submit yourselves therefore to God. Resist the devil, and he will flee from you. James 4:7

Chapter 13: Rebuking the devourer

Be sober, be vigilant; because your adversary the devil, as a roaring lion, walketh about, seeking whom he may devour: 1 Peter 5:8

Has this ever happened to you? Your car breaks down, your washing machine quits working, your air conditioning conks out, and your bank account is overdrawn, all on the same day?

The Bible has a solution to this.

Bring ye all the tithes into the storehouse, that there may be meat in mine house, and prove me now herewith, saith the LORD of hosts, if I will not open you the windows of heaven, and pour you out a blessing, that there shall not be room enough to receive it. And I will rebuke the devourer for your sakes, and he shall not destroy the fruits of your ground; neither shall your vine cast her fruit before the time in the field, saith the LORD of hosts. And all nations shall call you blessed: for ye shall be a delightsome land, saith the LORD of hosts. Malachi 3:10-12

Satan will devour everything you own, if you let him. He will take your money, your family, your job, your health, your peace and your joy. You will be left spiritually and physically exhausted, running around, trying to replenish what Satan has stolen from you.

Rather than trying to recover what has been stolen, wouldn't it be better if you could protect it in the first place? God's word says that tithing will protect what He has entrusted to you.

For those who are not familiar with the word tithe, it simply means one-tenth. If you are giving a tithe to your local church, you are giving one-tenth of your income.

I was shocked when I heard a preacher on the radio say that the tithe was not for today. This particular preacher said that Christians today didn't need to give a tithe; rather, they should just give whatever they felt was a good amount to give.

But God says that if you bring your tithes into the storehouse (your local church) He will bless you and rebuke the devourer (the devil).

Here is an example. I drove the same car for nineteen years. I was its second owner. When my sister blessed me with a beautiful new car, I donated the now twenty-one year old car to charity. It was still running great.

I never have to worry about things breaking down. Number one, they rarely break down, and number two, when they do, God always supernaturally provides the money to repair or replace them. And I don't mean VISA.

Why is this? Am I just a lucky person? There's no such thing as luck for Christians. Am I a millionaire? No. Do I have rich friends who just hand over money to me when I need it? That would be great, but, no.

The things that God has entrusted to me are protected because I learned the secret of tithing many years ago, and it has never failed me. It's hardly a secret, anyway – it is stated very plainly in these verses in Malachi.

Someone is thinking, "It can't be that easy. If I keep that ten percent and save it for a rainy day, I can use that money to repair my washing machine and my air conditioning when they break down."

That sounds logical on the surface, but human logic is no match for God's word. I have seen this happen time and time again: if you give ten percent of your income to the Lord, He stretches the remaining ninety percent, and it ends up going farther than if you had kept one hundred percent of it for yourself. I have also seen this happen: if you keep all of it, whatever you spent "your" money on will fail or be gone in short order.

Will a man rob God? Yet ye have robbed me. But ye say, Wherein have we robbed thee? In tithes and offerings. Ye are cursed with a curse: for ye have robbed me, even this whole nation. Malachi 3:8-9

News flash: ten percent of your income belongs to God. It's not yours! If you keep it, God says you are robbing Him.

It is absolutely amazing to me how many Christians resist tithing. Do you really want to work yourself to death, trying to replace everything that breaks down? Wouldn't you rather have a divine insurance policy that covers everything? All that you own is under warranty, and all you have to pay is the low, low premium – ten percent of your income. That is many more times a bargain than scrambling to come up with one hundred percent of the cost of a new refrigerator.

The concept of the tithe goes beyond money, in my opinion. I heard a man of God say once that there are twenty-four hours in one day, so we owe God about two hours and twenty-four minutes a day. What does that mean? Dedicate at least that much time to Him in prayer, service, singing, thanksgiving, etc.

It is exhausting to have to constantly work to buy new things, replace stolen things, repair broken things, etc. Along with these financial burdens comes a lot of worry and stress. I thank God for His insurance policy over my life, and His daily blessing and protection over me.

His lord said unto him, Well done, good and faithful servant; thou hast been faithful over a few things, I will make thee ruler over many things: enter thou into the joy of thy lord. Matthew 25:23

Chapter 14: Psychology

Verily, verily, I say unto you, He that entereth not by the door into the sheepfold, but climbeth up some other way, the same is a thief and a robber. But he that entereth in by the door is the shepherd of the sheep. To him the porter openeth; and the sheep hear his voice: and he calleth his own sheep by name, and leadeth them out. And when he putteth forth his own sheep, he goeth before them, and the sheep follow him: for they know his voice. And a stranger will they not follow, but will flee from him: for they know not the voice of strangers. John 10:1-5

A stranger isn't just someone that you don't know. A stranger, in this instance, means anyone who is telling you something contrary to the word of God. When you listen to, and act on, anything that is contrary to God's word, it will eventually result in spiritual exhaustion.

Psychology has almost completely infiltrated the church, and that is a sad commentary on the condition of the church today. I know I will offend many by saying this, but psychology and Christianity are two opposing world views. You are going to have to choose which one you want to believe, because you can't believe both. The underlying premise of psychology is that people are basically good; they just make bad choices from time to time.

Today we have something called "Christian psychologists" who attempt to blend psychology with the Bible. This results in a mixture of the profane and the holy.

Imagine making a delicious pot of soup for your family on a cold winter's day, then adding a handful of dirt to it, and stirring it in. This is what happens when people attempt to blend psychology and Christianity.

I was absolutely flabbergasted while listening to a psychologist on a very popular Christian radio program one morning. He was giving advice to women whose husbands were not doing what they wanted them to do. His advice? Stop cooking your husband's meals, stop doing his laundry, stop talking to him, stop sleeping with him, etc.

I have a habit of yelling at the radio, so I started yelling. "The Bible says if your enemy is hungry, feed him. If he's thirsty, give him something to drink (Romans 12:20). Where is your "advice" found in the Bible, Mr. Psychologist?" This episode was the deciding factor for me in no longer listening to this program.

In another instance, a friend of mine was having marital problems, and she went to her pastor for counsel. He told her that since her husband was not doing what he was supposed to be doing, it was okay for her to leave him.

A few questions: Have you ever failed to do what God wanted you to do? Have you ever broken His commandments, or disappointed Him?

Did He leave you as a result of your failure?

Don't listen to the voice of strangers.

Those in the church who have the gift of teaching are obligated to teach the congregation the ways of the Lord, what His word has to say, and what He expects of us. This is almost always the opposite of what the world and its psychologists recommend.

And they shall teach my people the difference between the holy and profane, and cause them to discern between the unclean and the clean. Ezekiel 44:23

What does the Bible have to say about the human race?

And God saw that the wickedness of man was great in the earth, and that every imagination of the thoughts of his heart was only evil continually. Genesis 6:5

Behold, I was shapen in iniquity; and in sin did my mother conceive me. Psalm 51:5

The heart is deceitful above all things, and desperately wicked: who can know it? Jeremiah 17:9

For I know that in me (that is, in my flesh,) dwelleth no good thing: for to will is present with me; but how to perform that which is good I find not. Romans 7:18

That's a far cry from being a "basically good" person who just messes up once in a while.

I have learned the hard way not to let others' actions influence my reactions. Yes, in a perfect world, my husband and everyone else would always do exactly what I want them to do, but since none of us live in that world, it is up to me to do the right thing, regardless of what others are doing.

It is not always easy to do the right thing!

If thou doest well, shalt thou not be accepted? and if thou doest not well, sin lieth at the door. Genesis 4:7a

This verse is talking about being accepted by God, not by human beings. If we do the right thing, He will accept us, and it is also true that if we do the right thing, people will often reject us.

In my book, *Winter in Eden* (2020, Giant Publishing Company) I discussed the dangers of listening to and following what other people say, rather than the voice of God. Unfortunately, many of us are people-pleasers. We can't stand the thought of being criticized, or being labeled insensitive, a hater, a bigot, an extremist, etc. We are definitely living in an upside-down world when someone who believes that only biological women should participate in women's sports is labeled a bigot.

I thank my God that He created me without the people-pleasing gene. I simply don't have it. It certainly makes life a lot easier.

Psychological counseling can be very harmful to a person who is seeking God's will for his or her life. These types of counselors will identify what your problem is, and to their credit, they are often right. But they rarely offer a biblical solution to your problem. In the case of my friend who I mentioned previously, the best advice that her psychologically-influenced pastor could give her was to leave her husband. And guess what? If she leaves her husband, it is a guarantee that the next person who comes into her life will also disappoint her, because people always disappoint us.

One definition of the word psychology is "the science of human and animal behavior." But you don't have to be a scientist to grasp human behavior.

The heart is deceitful above all things, and desperately wicked: who can know it? Jeremiah 17:9

Of course, no one enjoys being called wicked. But let's get real: our wickedness is the reason Jesus died on the cross.

Psychology may pinpoint your problem, but once it does, you will be labeled a victim. Everything that has gone wrong in your life is someone else's fault. To be sure, some of the things that have gone wrong in your life really are someone else's fault. But psychology will leave you in victim mode indefinitely. This is clearly seen in several of the social justice movements which are popular today. They focus on everything that has gone wrong in the past, and try to force those living their lives today to pay for the mistakes of their ancestors. Do black lives matter? Absolutely they do. Do all black lives matter? Not according to the BLM movement, a very strong proponent of abortion. They never mention that black babies are aborted at a much higher rate than white babies. Instead of being horrified by this, they continue to push abortion, while labeling their members as victims.

The #MeToo movement is very similar. Almost any woman can dredge up an incident from her past when she was harassed by a man. Rather than claiming victim status and demanding her rights, this woman can claim the rights that God has given her as His creation, and realize that as long as fallen human beings exist on this planet, harassment is going to occur, along with every other sin.

Rather than being victims for the rest of our lives, you and I need to reach up and take the hand of God. He will pull us out of the pit we are in, even if someone else threw us into it, and He will show us a new path to take and give us a new name: Victor, not Victim.

The most amazing and beautiful illustration of this is the life of Joseph. He is my favorite Bible character, hands down. God gave Joseph the gift of prophetic dreams, along with the interpretation of dreams. Joseph made the mistake of telling his brothers his dreams, which caused them to be jealous of him. That jealousy eventually turned into hatred. They at first plotted to kill him, then changed their minds and threw him into a pit instead. He ended up being sold into slavery, falsely accused of rape, and imprisoned for a crime he didn't commit.

I have often wondered if Joseph ever felt like a victim. The fact is, he was a victim. But the Bible tells us that Joseph looked to God when he was a slave, when he was falsely accused, and when he was in prison. The Bible does not record that Joseph ever asked, "God, why me? I have served You all my life, and this is what happens to me?" Instead, we see Joseph clinging to God and His promises in spite of the horrible circumstances he was in.

When Joseph was in prison, I wonder if he thought about the dreams he'd had when he was living with his family. I wonder if he thought they would never come true.

Joseph, more than anyone, had the right to label himself as a victim and to live his life with a victim mentality. But he didn't. God supernaturally plucked him out of prison, promoted him, and elevated him to become the second most important man in Egypt. When he was reunited with his family years later, this is what he said to them:

Now therefore be not grieved, nor angry with yourselves, that ye sold me hither: for God did send me before you to preserve life. But as for you, ye thought evil against me; but God meant it unto good, to bring to pass, as it is this day, to save much people alive. Genesis 45:5, Genesis 50:20

Joseph's story is an amazing account of transformation and forgiveness. He chose to believe God and His promises, and refused to allow himself to live like a victim.

The heart is deceitful above all things, and desperately wicked: who can know it? Jeremiah 17:9

Human beings are wicked. That means you, me, him and her. We need to understand that the root of all the evil and injustice in this world is human wickedness.

No psychologist will ever tell you that you are wicked. He or she will tell you that you are a victim of other people's bad behavior, or a victim of the way your parents raised you, or that you are really a good guy/gal, you've just made a few mistakes along the way (because, after all, we all make mistakes), and that will be $150.00, and see you next week.

It would be funny if it wasn't so sad.

For if any be a hearer of the word, and not a doer, he is like unto a man beholding his natural face in a glass: For he beholdeth himself, and goeth his way, and straightway forgetteth what manner of man he was. But whoso looketh into the perfect law of liberty, and continueth therein, he being not a forgetful hearer, but a doer of the work, this man shall be blessed in his deed. James 1:23 – 25

Pursuing psychology for the answer to your problems will exhaust you. It may help you identify the problems, but it offers no lasting solution for your problems. Pursue the word of God instead.

Happy is the man that findeth wisdom, and the man that getteth understanding. Proverbs 3:13

Get wisdom, get understanding: forget it not; neither decline from the words of my mouth. Proverbs 4:5

Wisdom is the principal thing; therefore get wisdom: and with all thy getting get understanding. Proverbs 4:7

How much better is it to get wisdom than gold! and to get understanding rather to be chosen than silver! Proverbs 16:16

He that getteth wisdom loveth his own soul: he that keepeth understanding shall find good. Proverbs 19:8

I have learned that the word of God contains the answer to every problem I have. That may seem simplistic to some, but it is the truth. If I pursue the word of God, He will not allow me to become spiritually exhausted.

But they that wait upon the LORD shall renew their strength; they shall mount up with wings as eagles; they shall run, and not be weary; and they shall walk, and not faint. Isaiah 40:31

Chapter 15: The latest thing

(For all the Athenians and strangers which were there spent their time in nothing else, but either to tell, or to hear some new thing.) Acts 17:21

Does this verse sound like some Christians you know? Do you have a friend who flies from conference to conference, looks for a prophet in every city, and moves from church to church? This type of lifestyle can be exciting, to be sure, but will always lead to spiritual exhaustion.

*That he would grant you, according to the riches of his glory, to be strengthened with might by his Spirit in the inner man; That Christ may dwell in your hearts by faith; that ye, being rooted and grounded in love...*Ephesians 3:16 – 17

God wants us to be rooted and grounded in love, and in our local church. Throughout the Bible, He compares us to plants and trees.

And he shall be like a tree planted by the rivers of water, that bringeth forth his fruit in his season; his leaf also shall not wither; and whatsoever he doeth shall prosper. Psalm 1:3

Thy wife shall be as a fruitful vine by the sides of thine house: thy children like olive plants round about thy table. Psalm 128:3

And these are they likewise which are sown on stony ground; who, when they have heard the word, immediately receive it with gladness; And have no root in themselves, and so endure but for a time: afterward, when affliction or persecution ariseth for the word's sake, immediately they are offended. Mark 4:16 – 17

It is impossible to grow and mature in the Lord if you are constantly uprooting yourself and re-planting yourself in a new place. Some people do this because they are easily offended – someone said something that they don't like (often it's the church leadership) – so they pick up and move elsewhere. Some people are restless and easily bored, so they look for a more exciting church. A friend of mine moves from church to church to church, and recently started driving about eighty miles to a church in another city, because she had exhausted all her options in our city.

My pastors say that such people are spiritual vagabonds. Like a homeless person moving from shelter to shelter, spiritual vagabonds move from church to church, never staying long enough to put down roots.

Plants will wither if you pull them up by the roots. At best, they will wilt for a short time, then eventually revive if they are re-planted in good soil. But if the process keeps repeating, the plant will eventually die. When roots are not planted in good soil, they are exposed to the elements, and the plant is no longer able to receive nourishment through its roots. Without good food, it dies.

It is important to root and ground yourself in the word of God. God has spoken to all of us, in one way or another. Once He has spoken, cling to what He has said and don't deviate from it.

For I am the LORD, I change not...Malachi 3:6a

There is nothing wrong with asking for confirmation from the Lord regarding what He has told you. But there is a serious problem with asking for seven confirmations and ten more prophecies, when you already know what God wants you to do.

It is easy to fall into this trap.

Now when John had heard in the prison the works of Christ, he sent two of his disciples, And said unto him, Art thou he that should come, or do we look for another? Matthew 11:2 – 3

This is the same John, John the Baptist, who had baptized Jesus earlier, and had experienced this:

The next day John seeth Jesus coming unto him, and saith, Behold the Lamb of God, which taketh away the sin of the world. John 1:29

When we determine in our hearts to follow Jesus, the going always gets tough. For John, it meant a prison sentence and eventual execution. John knew that Jesus was the Christ, the long-awaited Messiah, the anointed Son of the living God. But alone in that dark prison cell, he began to doubt.

Like John, when things start getting really tough, we start questioning what God has said. We start looking for some "new thing;" a new word, a new prophecy, a new experience, a new Bible study, or a new church. Sometimes people start looking for a new husband or wife.

God's word is supposed to be planted firmly in your heart and mine.

Thy word have I hid in mine heart, that I might not sin against thee. Psalm 119:11

Today, with so many social media platforms, people become spiritually exhausted flitting from one website to another, like manic butterflies. Everyone else seems to be more spiritual than you are. Everyone else seems to have a deeper insight into God and His word than you do.

My pastor said that the Jews stoned people that didn't follow the scriptures or preach the word in exactly the way the leaders thought they should. They, of course, used actual stones. Today, the stones people use are digital.

Here is an example. I was very broken-hearted when I read the online comments about a man of God who had recently died. After he died, conveniently, allegations were made against him of wrong-doing. "Everyone" had to chime in with their two cents' worth regarding this man, whether they thought he was guilty, innocent, or somewhere in between. And, predictably, those who disagreed with others' online comments began "stoning" each other on the websites where the comments were posted.

There are so many things about this scenario that are just plain wrong! Why wait until a person is dead to accuse him of something? He can no longer defend himself. If you believe a person is truly guilty, why not talk to him when he is still alive, and give him a chance to tell his side of the story? The fact that the accusations came after his death was highly suspicious to me. Matthew 18:15-17 tells us how to deal with wrongdoing in the church:

Moreover if thy brother shall trespass against thee, go and tell him his fault between thee and him alone: if he shall hear thee, thou hast gained thy brother. But if he will not hear thee, then take with thee one or two more, that in the mouth of two or three witnesses every word may be established. And if he shall neglect to hear them, tell it unto the church: but if he neglect to hear the church, let him be unto thee as an heathen man and a publican.

Since the biblical method was not followed in this instance, at least not as far as I could see, there was no way to know for sure if the man was guilty or innocent. Knowing that, why on earth would a believer then attack another believer for having a different opinion about this man's guilt or innocence? It would come down to whether you liked the person, or didn't. Those who liked him thought he was innocent; those who didn't, thought he was guilty.

Immersion in social media will exhaust anyone. By its very nature, it leads you down one rabbit hole after another. An hour after you start your research, you have forgotten what it was you were looking for in the first place.

How quickly people want to comment on the latest news! Is it really necessary to weigh in on the supposed guilt or innocence of a man or woman of God?

A fool uttereth all his mind: but a wise man keepeth it in till afterwards. Proverbs 29:11

When someone is falsely accused, and all the comments are tallied up – for and against – and the allegations are found to be unmerited, it's interesting that no one seems to remember all the so-called "proof" that people posted and commented on earlier. Like the book *1984*, when the government decided that yesterday's facts were today's fiction, they simply deleted the old facts, presented new facts, and the general populace accepted the new information and forgot what was said yesterday. With social media platforms, that is exactly the situation we are in today.

You and I rarely have the wisdom and insight needed from God to determine who is right and who is wrong in an online debate involving accusations against a brother or sister. As

Mark Twain said, "It's better to keep your mouth shut and be thought of as a fool, than to open it and remove all doubt."

For I am the LORD, I change not; therefore ye sons of Jacob are not consumed. Malachi 3:6

Jesus Christ the same yesterday, and to day, and for ever. Hebrews 13:8

No matter what the latest social media trend is, no matter who is currently being stoned and who is being praised, aren't you glad that God doesn't change?

Chapter 16: Speaking the word of God

Through faith we understand that the worlds were framed by the word of God, so that things which are seen were not made of things which do appear. Hebrews 11:3

Did you know that you can frame your world by the words you speak? It's true. One of my biggest regrets is not learning this truth earlier in my life.

As believers, we have a solemn responsibility over every word we speak. For the biggest part of my life, I was exhausting myself without even knowing it, by the inaccurate and negative things I told myself and listened to.

But I say unto you, That every idle word that men shall speak, they shall give account thereof in the day of judgment. Matthew 12:36

Have you ever heard a parent say these types of things to a child?

"You'll never amount to anything."

"You're an idiot."

"You're not smart enough/pretty enough/strong enough to do that."

"I wish you were never born," or, "You were an accident."

It's hard to believe that parents could speak that way to a child. But they do. And guess what? If you tell your child those things, sure enough, your child will never amount to anything, will never be "enough," and will live his/her life as an accident waiting to happen.

Some parents have the mistaken idea that if they praise their child, he/she will get a big head and become obnoxiously conceited. So, praise is measured out with an eyedropper, if at all. It should surprise no one that without praise and positive words from our parents, we will rarely succeed.

I was commiserating with a friend of mine about this subject. She and I were raised in similar households. As for me, I could not remember a time that my parents had congratulated me for getting an A on my report card, or for an art award that I had won, or for being chosen to sing a solo in choir. As the British say, it simply wasn't done. I particularly remember as a teenager telling my mother that I would like to be a writer someday, and her immediate response: "You'll never do that."

Why are our words so important? Because we can literally create life or death with what we say.

Death and life are in the power of the tongue: and they that love it shall eat the fruit thereof. Proverbs 18:21

If you are going through a time of spiritual exhaustion, it is very important for you to examine the words you are saying, as well as the words you are listening to. Are you telling yourself that you'll never make it? Are you telling yourself that you are too dumb, uneducated, ugly, fat, poor, lazy, etc., to do the things that you want to do? Are your parents, your spouse, your friends, enemies, or frenemies, telling you that you don't have what it takes?

I'd like to let you in on a little secret.

You don't have what it takes. But Jesus does.

When my first book was finished, I was in the process of uploading it to the website where it would be offered for sale. One thing after another went wrong. After the seventh upload attempt failed, I gave up. (Giving up has been a life-long pattern for me.) I went to bed that night, telling God that I was sorry, but I just couldn't finish the job He gave me to do. I had no doubt that the book I had written was from God. I had no doubt that He wanted me to finish the book and publish it. But I couldn't seem to overcome all the obstacles that were standing in my way. And, after all, it really wasn't my fault, because if God wanted me to publish this book, surely the process would be all smooth sailing, wouldn't it?

No, it wouldn't. When we do what God has asked us to do, far from smooth sailing, we almost always encounter rough seas. In my case, the problem really wasn't the difficulty I was having with uploading my book. The problem was the lies the enemy was telling me, and I was believing. He was having a field day – whispering that I was a fool for thinking I could ever be a writer, and my lack of success in getting the book uploaded was surely "proof "of that.

But God is so merciful. After I slept on it, I awakened with a new resolve from the Holy Spirit to try once again to upload the book. And finally, I succeeded. The book that I was so ready to give up on is the same book that later won a national award.

God has used this incident and others like it to show me, time and again, that it is not I who has the talent, skills, ability, brainpower, or muscle to accomplish anything, but that it is He who is accomplishing His purpose, through me. I am a tool in the hands of the Lord.

I can do all things through Christ which strengtheneth me.
Philippians 4:13

When God told Nehemiah to rebuild the broken walls of Jerusalem, he encountered one obstacle after another. These obstacles were not a lack of materials or man power. They were negative words.

But it so happened, when Sanballat heard that we were rebuilding the wall, that he was furious and very indignant, and mocked the Jews. And he spoke before his brethren and the army of Samaria, and said, "What are these feeble Jews doing? Will they fortify themselves? Will they offer sacrifices? Will they complete it in a day? Will they revive the stones from the heaps of rubbish—stones that are burned?" Nehemiah 4:1-2 (New King James Version)

Now it happened, when Sanballat, Tobiah, the Arabs, the Ammonites, and the Ashdodites heard that the walls of Jerusalem were being restored and the gaps were beginning to be closed, that they became very angry, and all of them conspired together to come and attack Jerusalem and create confusion. Nehemiah 4:7-8 (New King James Version)

Then Sanballat sent his servant to me as before, the fifth time, with an open letter in his hand. In it was written: It is reported among the nations, and Geshem says, that you and the Jews plan to rebel; therefore, according to these rumors, you are rebuilding the wall, that you may be their king. And you have also appointed prophets to proclaim concerning you at Jerusalem, saying, "There is a king in Judah!" Now these matters will be reported to the king. So come, therefore, and let us consult together. Then I sent to him, saying, "No such things as you say are being done, but you invent them in your own heart." For they all were trying

92

to make us afraid, saying, "Their hands will be weakened in the work, and it will not be done." Now therefore, O God, strengthen my hands. Nehemiah 6:5-9 (New King James Version)

As I stated before, Satan has a very old playbook, and his tricks never vary. First, he used Nehemiah's enemies to ridicule him and try to make him believe he didn't have the ability to rebuild the wall. When that didn't work, he threatened Nehemiah with violence. When that failed, he tried to rattle Nehemiah by spreading false rumors about him. As Nehemiah said, the goal was to make them so afraid that they would give up. But Nehemiah responded to the enemy's lies with this prayer:

Now therefore, O God, strengthen my hands.

When you are in the middle of a spiritual attack, you need reinforcements. God will never call you to do something and then abandon you halfway. When you are ready to give up, pray along with Nehemiah, "O God, strengthen my hands."

It is vitally important for you to surround yourself with people who will speak life to you, not death. God has given you a dream and a purpose for your existence. That dream and purpose must be nurtured and cared for, like a baby growing in the womb. Do not allow any human being to speak death over you. If necessary, walk away, even if that person is your own mother. We should never deliberately try to be rude or antagonistic toward others, but when someone is telling you 'no' when God has said 'yes,' always go with what God has said!

I stated earlier that giving up has been a life-long pattern for me. Through a series of life-changing events, I had to come face to face with some very unpleasant facts about myself.

God had given me multiple assignments throughout my life, and I had failed to carry out any of them. I had always started out with good intentions, but always quit somewhere along the way – always when I hit an obstacle, or when a human being told me I couldn't or shouldn't be doing what I was doing. I have a lot of regret for failing God in this way, and for all the wasted years, but I also know I cannot live my life in regret. You shouldn't, either.

What has God called you to do? What stage are you in? Are you just starting out? Have you hit an obstacle? Are there people in your life who are using their words to kill the dream God has put in your heart?

Are their words making you spiritually exhausted?

My friend, there is hope. If you are at the end of your spiritual rope, try to get alone with God. Take a weekend, or a couple of days alone, and spend it with your heart and your Bible open. Come to Him with humility and repentance. Ask Him to forgive you for your failure to believe the words He's told you, and your tendency to prefer the words of others over the words of God. We have all done this; you are certainly not alone!

Examine yourselves as to whether you are in the faith. Test yourselves. Do you not know yourselves, that Jesus Christ is in you? - unless indeed you are disqualified. But I trust that you will know that we are not disqualified. 2 Corinthians 13:5-6 (New King James Version)

You are not disqualified! God has a unique purpose for you. He created each one of us to fulfil His plan, and His plan for me is not the same as His plan for you.

After you have taken stock of your situation, and repented if necessary, accept His forgiveness and give yourself a fresh start. It helps to write down your vision – what He has called you to do, and the steps you are going to take to get there. Remember to write down what God has already done for you! When you re-read this in the future, your faith will be strengthened.

But remember, things don't always go according to plan! There will be obstacles along the way – probably many. There's nothing wrong with making adjustments to the plan as you go along, as long as you remain with God's vision and don't substitute your own.

Pray along with me: "Dear Lord, I thank You for creating me for Your purpose. Open my eyes to see that purpose. Open my eyes to see the attacks that the enemy is launching against me. Help me to remember Who You are, and to remember Your word. Help me to block out every negative word spoken against me and Your plans for me. Strengthen my hands, oh God, to do the work that You have called me to do. In Jesus' mighty name, amen."

I trust that this book has blessed you. It has blessed me as well! Please visit our website for more resources:

www.giantpublishingcompany.com

www.ingramcontent.com/pod-product-compliance
Lightning Source LLC
Chambersburg PA
CBHW072206090426
42740CB00012B/2413